A·Q·U·A·M·A·S·T·E·R
— Stuart Thraves • Peter Hiscock • Gina Sandford —

Freshwater
AQUARIUMS

BOWTIE
P R E S S®
A Division of BowTie, Inc.
Laguna Hills, California

First published in the USA and Canada by BowTie Press®

A Division of BowTie, Inc.

23172 Plaza Pointe Drive, Suite 230

Laguna Hills, CA 92653

www.bowtiepress.com

Originally published in 2007

© 2007 Interpet Publishing

Vincent Lane

Dorking, Surrey

RH4 3YX, England

Library of Congress Cataloging-in-Publication Data

Thraves, Stuart, 1970–

Freshwater aquariums / Stuart Thraves, Peter Hiscock, Gina Sandford.

p. cm. — (Aquamaster)

ISBN 978-1-933958-08-8

1. Aquariums. 2. Aquarium fish. I. Hiscock, Peter. II. Sandford, Gina. III. Title.

SF457.3.T479 2007

639.34—dc22

2007009713

Created and compiled: Ideas into Print, Claydon, Suffolk, IP6 0AB, England

Design and prepress: Phil Kay Design, Elmdon, Saffron Walden, Essex CB11 4LT, England

Computer graphics: Phil Holmes and Stuart Watkinson

Principal photography: Geoffrey Rogers

© Interpet Publishing

Production management: Consortium, Poslingford, Suffolk CO10 8RA, England

Print production: Sino Publishing House Ltd., Hong Kong.

Printed and bound in China

10 09 08 07   1 2 3 4 5 6 7 8 9 10

Additional material supplied by Steve Halls.

Contents

Getting started

The first thing to bear in mind when buying an aquarium is that it must provide the correct conditions for your fish to survive. Like us, fish breathe in oxygen and exhale carbon dioxide. These gases are dissolved in the water and get in and out at the surface. Therefore, any aquarium must provide a large surface area to allow sufficient exchange of gases. Choose a location for your tank that will present a focal point in the room, is close to a power supply, and is convenient for carrying out essential routine maintenance.

SUITABLE TANKS

◀ Cube-shaped tanks have an acceptable surface area.

◀ This curved tank on its own stand comes with lighting and filtration equipment included.

◀ A rectangular aquarium is a traditional choice.

SITING THE AQUARIUM

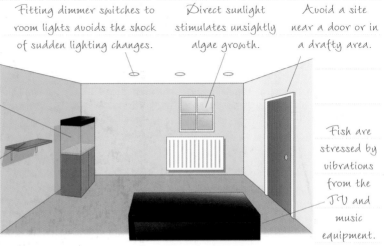

This is the ideal corner location. Electrical sockets should be nearby.

Fitting dimmer switches to room lights avoids the shock of sudden lighting changes.

Direct sunlight stimulates unsightly algae growth.

Avoid a site near a door or in a drafty area.

A bookshelf is not strong enough to support a y tank.

Fish are stressed by vibrations from the TV and music equipment.

STOCKING LEVELS

Tank volume determines how many fish you can keep. An initial stocking guide is about 1 in. (2.5 cm) of fish length, excluding tails, per 1.25 gal (4.5 L) of tank water volume. But this applies only to average-size fish (up to 1.5 in. or 4 cm in length) in normally proportioned tanks. Weight-to-length ratio rises significantly after that, and larger fish produce more waste; this means that, say, a 12 in. (30.5 cm) oscar needs more room than do 12 neon tetras each measuring 1 in. (about 2.5 cm) long.

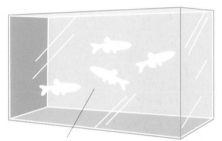

47.25x11.75x11.75 in. (120x30x30 cm) tank with four 6 in. (15 cm) fish

47.25x11.75x11.75 in. (120x30x30 cm) tank with twelve 2 in. (5 cm) fish

▶ Small "complete package" aquariums of about 5.25 gal (20 L) are a good introduction to fish keeping but are suitable for only a few small fish, such as neon tetras and zebra danios.

* Aim to buy the biggest aquarium you can afford and accommodate. The larger the volume of water, the easier it is to control the waste products and thus provide a stable environment.

▶ This table provides a guide to the capacity of a range of standard tanks. Multiply length (L) x breadth (B) x depth (D) in inches (centimeters) and divide by 231 (1,000) for the volume in gallons (liters). Reduce the volume by about 10% to allow for tank decor.

TANK SIZES AND CAPACITIES

Tank size (LxBxD)	Volume of water
23.5x11.75x11.75 in. (60x30x30 cm)	14.5 gallons (55 liters)
23.5x11.75x15 in. (60x30x38 cm)	18 gallons (68 liters)
35.5x11.75x11.75 in. (90x30x30 cm)	21.5 gallons (82 liters)
35.5x11.75x15 in. (90x30x38 cm)	27.5 gallons (104 liters)
47.25x11.75x11.75 in. (12x30x30 cm)	28.75 gallons (109 liters)
47.25x11.75x15 in. (120x30x38 cm)	36 gallons (136 liters)

Getting started (continued)

The height at which your aquarium is situated depends on several factors. If most of your viewing is from a seated position, the tank should ideally be at or just above eye level. Your own height and arm length should be considered too—you need to be able to reach down into the tank for maintenance without standing on a chair or step stool, which could be dangerous. If you plan to house the aquarium in an alcove or room divider, make sure there is access for cleaning and room to open the hood fully.

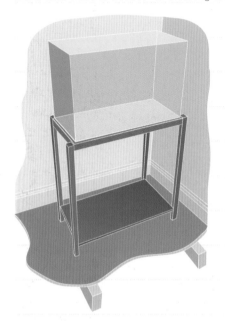

◀ *Concrete floors should easily support even the largest aquariums, but on a wooden floor, try to position the stand or cabinet so that the weight is borne by the joists (identifiable by the securing nails) rather than by the floorboards alone. Beware of placing anything other than the smallest tank upstairs; the ceiling may not take its weight.*

* *Before you order a large aquarium, check that your doors are wide enough to allow it access and that there is sufficient room to maneuver it into its final position. A tape measure will give you some clues, but a dummy run with a cardboard box of the same dimensions is more reassuring!*

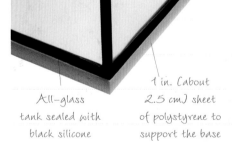

All-glass
tank sealed with
black silicone

1 in. (about
2.5 cm) sheet
of polystyrene to
support the base

▲ *Cushion an unframed, all-glass tank on its supporting cabinet or stand with a 1 in. (about 2.5 cm) sheet of polystyrene or plastic foam mat to iron out any irregularities.*

◀ *If the tank has a bottom frame that holds the glass base clear of the stand, there is no need to use a cushioning sheet.*

BACKGROUND OPTIONS

There are many background options available, ranging from black and blue to printed designs that simulate planted scenes, rocks, and tree roots. Cut the background to size before attaching it, and if you are using a picture background, trim it to show the best part of the design.

▲ Use themed backgrounds with care—they can look too gaudy.

◀ Secure the background to the outside glass before you move the tank against the wall and fill it; otherwise, the aquarium will be too heavy to move.

* Think about the sort of fish you would like to keep, and find out as much as you can about them, as this will affect how you set up your tank. For example, tall fish, such as discus, require a deep tank, shoaling fish will need plenty of swimming space, and shy species must have some suitable retreats.

◀ Kissing gouramis (Helostoma temminckii) grow up to 11.75 in. (30 cm) in the wild, but only half this in the aquarium. Keep just two or three as adults with other fish.

▼ For color and activity in the aquarium, consider keeping a shoal of red phantom tetras (Megalamphodus sweglesi). These peaceful fish from the Amazon Basin swim mainly in the lower levels.

Aquarium substrates

The substrate creates a natural bed within the aquarium and supports any rocks and wood that you add as part of the decor. However, its main function is to anchor and nourish the plant roots that will grow through it. Many different substrates are available for aquarium use, including pea gravel, quartz gravel, and sand. Lava rock, in small-grade particles up to 0.1 in. (3 mm), makes an ideal aquarium substrate. Unfortunately, most aquarium substrates do not contain any nutrients and cannot sustain plant growth on their own. The solution is to add a long-term food supplement, such as laterite, in conjunction with a bacterial culture that will release the nutrients in a form that plants can use.

TYPES OF SUBSTRATE

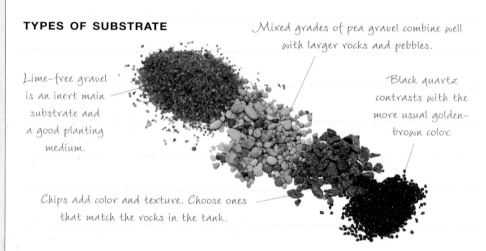

Mixed grades of pea gravel combine well with larger rocks and pebbles.

Lime-free gravel is an inert main substrate and a good planting medium.

Black quartz contrasts with the more usual golden-brown color.

Chips add color and texture. Choose ones that match the rocks in the tank.

A HEATER CABLE

If you plan to include live plants in your aquarium, then a heating cable placed beneath the substrate can provide a gentle warmth to encourage and sustain healthy root and plant growth. The model shown here is designed for use with aquarium plants. Connect the low-wattage cable to the transformer, and position this in a dry place outside the aquarium.

◀ The coil of heating wire is housed in a plastic sleeve.

▲ The cable sits on the tank base.

▲ Lava rock has an open structure and supports plant roots.

*A dark substrate can have a striking effect, showing plants, fish, and decor better than lighter substrates do. Look through the colored gravels to find the more subtle browns, grays, dark reds, and blacks. Many fish find a darker substrate more relaxing, resulting in lower stress levels and better overall health and color.

USING SAND

Silver sand is a good medium for placing over a heating cable, as it distributes heat evenly while holding the cable securely in position. However, it compacts and can stagnate in time, turning black and releasing toxins. Plant roots help keep this from happening, but in open areas, agitate the sand gently with your fingers once or twice a week. Sand is best used as a base layer.

▲ If you are keeping scavenging fish, such as bottom-dwelling loaches and catfish, avoid sharp or jagged substrates and rocks. These fish can easily damage themselves on unsuitable decor and succumb to bacterial infections.

▲ Wash all but specially designed substrates in several changes of tap water before adding them to the tank. Do not try to clean the material all at once; instead, place a small amount in the water, and agitate it until the water runs clear.

▲ You can choose a substrate that reflects a particular environment. Here, a mixture of gravels and small pebbles emulates a streambed.

AQUARIUM SUBSTRATES

Aquarium furnishings

Bogwood and bamboo are popular items of decor that simulate natural features from various habitats around the world. The safest option is to buy bogwood from an aquarium shop, as you can be sure that it will be suitable for underwater use. Wood from other sources may quickly rot and release chemicals that are potentially harmful to fish. Bogwood is available in many sizes, shapes, and colors. Choose pieces that resemble tree roots and stumps, as these look more natural in an aquarium display. You can also use pieces of bogwood to hide aquarium equipment, such as an internal filter.

TYPES OF WOOD

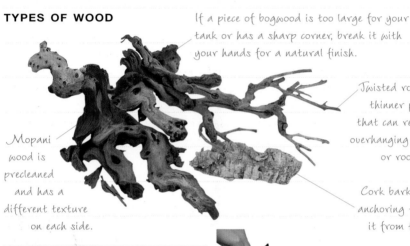

If a piece of bogwood is too large for your tank or has a sharp corner, break it with your hands for a natural finish.

Twisted roots are thinner pieces that can represent overhanging branches or roots.

Mopani wood is precleaned and has a different texture on each side.

Cork bark will need anchoring to prevent it from floating.

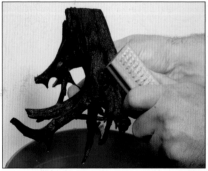

◀ Prepare bogwood by submerging it in a deep bucket of clean water.

▶ After several days, the water starts to discolor.

▲ Brush the bogwood to remove dirt and debris. Wet it to remove stubborn marks, and use a smaller brush to get into narrow crevices.

◀ When the water looks likes strong tea, replace it with fresh water. Repeat until the water is clear.

▶ *The shape and rough texture of Mopani wood, a type of bogwood, are reminiscent of fallen branches. The natural cave formed by the wood will be a welcome retreat for fish. Embed decor securely.*

Bamboo is a striking material that can provide excellent cover for many aquarium fish. It is available in various diameters at aquatic dealers and garden centers. You can seal bamboo with the clear plastic paint normally sold for sealing concrete ponds. This not only prevents any harmful substances from leaching into the aquarium but also keeps the wood from rotting. Several coats may be required to achieve a good seal. The chunky texture of cork bark can be almost rocklike, and some plants, such as *Anubias*, will readily grow on it.To anchor bamboo or cork bark, you may need to attach it to a piece of glass.

▶ *Attaching small pieces of bark to a piece of glass with silicone prevents them from floating. Placed on the aquarium floor, they appear to make a long, but fragmented, line.*

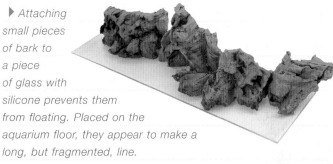

▲ *Left untreated, bamboo will rot in the aquarium, releasing organic elements that may cause algal or fungal blooms. Allow it to dry out completely before painting it with a sealant suitable for aquarium use.*

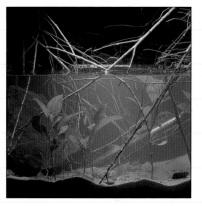

◀ *Thin, twiglike brushwood makes realistic decor, as long as there are no living parts left. To test it, break open the thickest part. If it bends rather than snaps or contains any green material, discard it. Soak it before use.*

Aquarium furnishings (continued)

Aquarium stores carry a selection of rocks, but not all of them are suitable for the freshwater tropical displays we are considering in this book. As with the substrate, choose inert materials that will not alter water chemistry, such as basalt, flint, slate, sandstone, quartz, and lava rock. Avoid calcareous materials such as limestone, marble, and chalk.

TYPES OF ROCK

Westmorland rock has red markings.

Granite has an unusual sparkling texture.

Slate is available in a range of shapes and sizes.

Rounded boulders make good grazing spots for algae eaters.

Small rounded pebbles create a riverbed.

Chips of many rock types are available. These are slate pieces.

Broken pieces of lava rock create an unusual substrate.

Washed coal creates a darker display.

TESTING ROCKS

To test if a rock is likely to alter the water chemistry, pour on some acidic substance such as vinegar. If the rock contains any calcareous substances, it will begin to fizz gently. If there is no fizzing, it should be safe to use in the aquarium.

◀ *Rocks are usually dirty and dusty and may harbor mosses and lichens that could foul the water. Scrub them (no soap) before adding them to the tank. Clean, wet rock shows its true colors under aquarium lighting.*

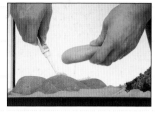

▶ *When you have decided where the rocks are to go, use silicone to glue them into place. Squeeze large beads of silicone onto any hard, clean surface.*

◀ *Fill any gaps between the rocks with more silicone. Do not worry if the silicone is visible; it can be trimmed away quite easily when it is dry.*

▲ *To make a lava rock cave, select two pieces of rock for the base and apply sealant. Firmly press on the roof.*

ARTIFICIAL DECOR

This fake bark is a good shape for hiding filters.

Synthetic rock is inert and safe in the aquarium.

Artificial wood looks natural and does not alter the color of the water.

Fake wood is available in manageable sizes.

▲ *Combining artificial pieces of decor with genuine rocks and plants help them appear more authentic. In this display, the rocks and pebbles are real but the wood is synthetic.*

AQUASCAPING TIPS

- Rock strata should run in the same direction, ideally horizontally.
- Smaller pieces of rock or wood can divide plant-growing areas.
- Individual cobbles, pebbles, and stones made good aquarium decor, but used together, they have greater impact.
- Leave some empty space for the plants to grow and for the fish to swim.
- Get ideas from books, magazines, and dealers' show tanks.

Aquarium plants

Before proceeding with any planting, it is worthwhile to sketch out a basic plan of the aquarium and mark where the plants are to go. As a guide, identify the background, midground, and foreground areas, and consider having a tall plant at each of the front corners to achieve a natural tiered effect. Leave enough room for each plant to grow, then make a list of the species you would like to include.

A PLANTING PLAN FOR THE AQUARIUM

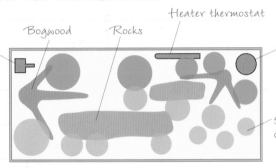

Mark the position of tank equipment, such as a water pump for a CO_2 system to promote healthy plant growth.

Bogwood   Rocks   Heater thermostat

Internal filter

Use plants in groups of three or more for the best effect.

 Background   Midground   ◯ Foreground

CHOOSING HEALTHY PLANTS

◀ Leaves with no holes, plus roots and small plantlets growing through the base of the pot, are evidence of a healthy plant.

▶ Avoid plants with brown or damaged leaves. They will rot away in the aquarium. Yellow patches indicate a lack of nutrients.

* Buying plants from a retailer enables you to pick out the species you need and examine individual specimens. However, the range of plants may be limited.

▲ For a greater choice, consider buying mail order plants. They should arrive separately wrapped and in good condition. Check the plants against your order.

PREPARING POTTED PLANTS

1 Remove the container. Cut the sides until you can remove the plant wrapped in rockwool.

2 Remove as much rockwool as you can without damaging the roots; they should be white and strong.

3 If the roots are too long, trim them with sharp scissors so you can spread them out when planting.

4 Remove any old or damaged leaves. Make sure there are no snails or signs of their eggs.

▶ *If the roots are very fine, expose only the base, and leave the remaining rockwool intact.*

* *Most potted plants are grown in a rockwool medium to support the roots while they are in the nursery. Once they are planted in the aquarium, they will obtain their nutrients from the substrate, so before planting, remove as much rockwool as possible from the roots.*

* *Bunched plants are often held together with lead strips. Discard these, and separate the individual plants before planting them in groups.*

▶ *Some aquatic plants, such as Java fern, prefer to be planted on wood and porous rocks, rather than in the substrate. Set the plant on some bogwood in a natural position. Attach the root firmly but gently to the wood with black cotton thread.*

Lighting the aquarium

Most standard aquariums use fluorescent lighting, which is widely available. Use only aquatic lighting tubes; domestic lights are unsuitable and potentially dangerous. Aquatic fluorescent tubes are designed with a specific purpose. Some promote plant growth; others will bring out the colors of the fish. It is possible to combine different tubes to achieve certain effects. Fluorescent tubes are very cheap to buy and run. However, they radiate in all directions and bounce light around the hood instead of down into the aquarium. This can be resolved by fitting an inexpensive reflector that directs the maximum amount of light downward.

HOW PLANTS USE LIGHT IN THE AQUARIUM

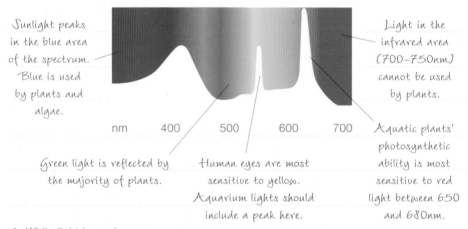

Sunlight peaks in the blue area of the spectrum. Blue is used by plants and algae.

Light in the infrared area (700–750nm) cannot be used by plants.

nm   400   500   600   700

Green light is reflected by the majority of plants.

Human eyes are most sensitive to yellow. Aquarium lights should include a peak here.

Aquatic plants' photosynthetic ability is most sensitive to red light between 650 and 680nm.

▲ White light is made up of different wavelengths, each corresponding to a specific color. Plants use only some of the light they receive, concentrating on specific areas of the spectrum and using only certain wavelengths, usually those that are most readily available. Chlorophyll uses mostly blue and red light.

* Wavelengths of light are measured in nanometers (nm) — billionths of a meter.

◀ For a balanced light output in the aquarium, choose a fluorescent tube with the three required peaks of blue, red, and yellow. These are best produced by a triphosphor tube. A pink tube will enhance plant growth.

POWER COMPACT TUBES

Power compact fluorescent tubes are, in effect, traditional tubes bent in two with all the fittings at one end. They have a higher power rating—up to 96 watts—and therefore an increased light output suitable to penetrate to the depths of most home aquariums. They are smaller than traditional tubes, allowing more tubes to be fitted in the same size aquarium hood. And finally, the two halves of the U-shaped lamp can be coated with different phosphors, allowing two different light mixes to be emitted from a single unit.

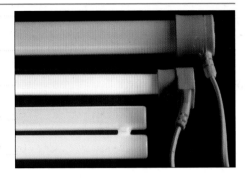

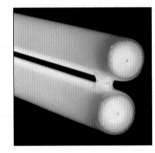

▲ *Power compact tube compared with normal style tubes*

◀ *These tubes produce an intense light.*

METAL-HALIDE LIGHTING

Metal-halide lamps are much more expensive than fluorescent tubes but produce a great deal of light; they are available in 70-watt bulbs. Most fittings have built-in reflectors that direct all the light downward to illuminate deep aquariums and provide the brightness levels needed to satisfy even the most demanding aquarium plants. Because metal-halide lamps are so powerful, they also run very hot. Use them only over open-topped aquariums. This allows the lights to keep cool but increases evaporation from the water surface, possibly causing unwanted condensation elsewhere in the home.

▲ *Metal-halide lamps for aquarium use are fitted into housings such as this one and suspended above the open tank.*

* The stark lighting produced by metal-halide lamps can create an impressive mix of bright focal points and pockets of deep shade, welcomed by fish that appreciate cover away from intense light. Available as suspended units, these lights are also sold as overtank lighting units raised up on slim brackets.

Carbon dioxide fertilization

For plants to flourish in the aquarium, they need sufficient levels of dissolved carbon dioxide gas (CO_2) to use in photosynthesis to make glucose for energy and growth. In a natural aquatic habitat, the respiration of other living organisms (including bacteria) produces enough carbon dioxide gas as a waste product to sustain photosynthesis. However, in the enclosed environment of an aquarium, there is not enough respiration taking place to maintain sufficiently high CO_2 levels for optimum photosynthetic activity. Adding carbon dioxide gas directly to the water makes up for this shortfall.

A CARBON DIOXIDE GENERATOR

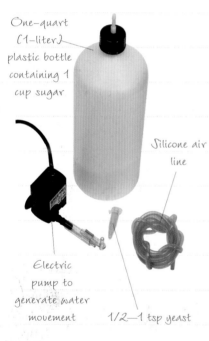

One-quart (1-liter) plastic bottle containing 1 cup sugar

Silicone air line

Electric pump to generate water movement

1/2—1 tsp yeast

1 Add warm water to the reactor bottle to dissolve the sugar.

2 Replace the cap and shake the bottle well.

3 Add the yeast to the sugar solution to start the fermentation process.

4 Connect the silicone air line to the special cap of the reactor bottle.

▲ *This simple fertilization kit meets the CO_2 needs of plants in a medium-size aquarium (up to 39.5 gallons [150 liters]). It operates at low pressure and produces small bubbles. The system is effective and highly controllable—a vital consideration when adding CO_2 gas to the aquarium.*

* Too little CO_2 will not benefit plants; too much can be lethal to fish.

INTRODUCING CO₂ GAS

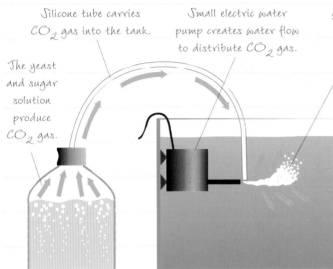

Silicone tube carries CO₂ gas into the tank.

Small electric water pump creates water flow to distribute CO₂ gas.

Gentle streams of gas bubbles flow into the water.

The yeast and sugar solution produce CO₂ gas.

To prevent back siphoning in the event of a power cut, either place the reactor bottle above the aquarium water level or fit a check valve in the silicone tubing carrying the gas to the tank.

▲ The unit will start to produce CO₂ gas in about 24 hours, lasting up to six weeks before a refill kit of sugar and blended yeasts is needed.

* Ensure that CO₂ dosing occurs only when the lights are on and the plants are actively photosynthesizing.

CO₂ CYLINDER FERTILIZATION

▶ For larger aquariums, the best option is to use a carbon dioxide dosing system based on bottles of pressurized gas. Such a setup can support vigorous plant growth for months at a time before the gas bottles need refilling (by your aquarium dealer).

Valve closes when lights are off.

Cylinder system is connected to a light timer.

The cylinder contains compressed CO₂ gas, released at a controlled rate via a regulator.

Aquarium lights provide an energy source for photosynthesis.

Tiny CO₂ bubbles travel slowly upward through a bubble counter, allowing maximum time for the gas to diffuse into the water.

Filtration

All aquarium filters are designed to perform the same basic tasks—to remove solid waste from the water and provide a large surface area bathed with oxygenated water that will stimulate the growth of millions of beneficial cleansing bacteria. A third task is to remove specific wastes or toxic products from the water with chemical filter media. There is a wide choice of filters on the market. An internal power filter sits discreetly in the back corner of the aquarium. A submersible water pump at the top of the unit draws water through the filter medium and circulates it back into the tank. The filter medium is a simple block of open cell plastic foam that performs the twin tasks of trapping solid debris from the water flow and providing a large surface area for beneficial bacteria.

AN INTERNAL POWER FILTER

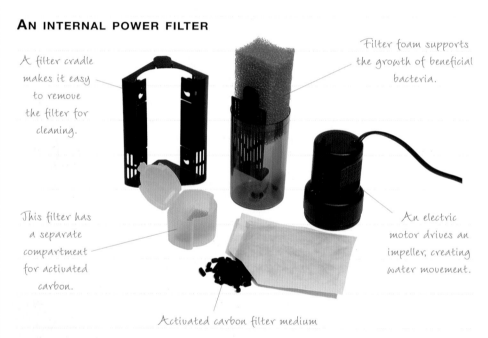

A filter cradle makes it easy to remove the filter for cleaning.

Filter foam supports the growth of beneficial bacteria.

This filter has a separate compartment for activated carbon.

An electric motor drives an impeller, creating water movement.

Activated carbon filter medium

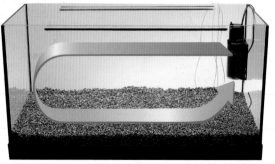

◀ Dirty water is drawn into the filter at the base, so be sure to position the unit well above the substrate. Once cleaned, the water returns to the tank via the nozzle at the top, which should face diagonally outward.

An external filter is located outside the aquarium. Being generally larger than an internal filter, it can house different types of media for mechanical, biological, and chemical filtration. These are often housed in separate compartments inside the filter body.

AN EXTERNAL POWER FILTER

Dirty water enters the filter by gravity, is cleaned, and then is pumped back to the aquarium.

Ceramic cylinders provide the biological medium on which beneficial bacteria can multiply.

An internal canister houses the different filter media arranged in layers.

Filter foam traps large pieces of debris and acts as a biological medium.

Activated carbon removes toxic substances.

Filter wool prevents fine particles from becoming trapped in the impeller.

▼ *Arrange the filter media in the canister with the coarse filter foam at the bottom, followed by a layer of biological medium, then carbon, and finally a wad of filter wool.*

AIR-POWERED FILTERS

Air-powered sponge filters are safe to use in quarantine/hospital aquariums or fry-rearing tanks. They not only trap dirt particles, but they are also colonized by micro-organisms that provide live food for young fish. However, they are not suitable for a main aquarium of any kind.

FILTRATION

Filtration (continued)

Mechanical filter media range from various grades of foam to very fine filter wool. Biological filtration media include sintered glass and ceramic cylinders. Chemical media are used as short-term solutions to water quality problems by removing toxic substances from the aquarium.

▲ Filter foam doubles as a mechanical and biological filtration medium. Clean it regularly in water from the aquarium to ensure that it does not become clogged.

▲ Sintered glass is a high-capacity biological filter medium. It is best used together with excellent mechanical filtration because a buildup of solid debris in the water will render it useless.

▲ Alfagrog is a porous, inert, ceramic material that supports a healthy population of beneficial bacteria. Common in the UK, it can be used as a planting substrate.

▲ Gravel was once widely used as a filter medium but has been surpassed by more efficient materials.

▲ Activated carbon blended from a variety of sources is the most effective form for general aquarium use.

▲ *Filter floss removes fine particles and "polishes" the water before it is finally returned to the tank. Check it regularly and replace it when it becomes clogged.*

CHEMICAL FILTER MEDIA

These are usually specific ion-exchange resins that pick up a particular chemical in the water, such as nitrate or phosphate, and swap it for a harmless salt. Always use such media along with a test kit to monitor the levels of the chemical you are trying to eliminate.

HEATING THE AQUARIUM

The combined submersible heater-thermostat (heaterstat) is simple to regulate but not easy to tamper with once set at the correct temperature and installed in the tank. Most heaterstats are supplied preset at 80.6°F (27°C). To alter the temperature, simply turn the adjuster knob at the top of the unit. To determine the required heater wattage for an aquarium, use an approximate guideline of 4 watts per gallon (1 watt per liter) of tank volume. Round up from this figure to the nearest heater size.

For larger aquariums, consider splitting the total required heater wattages between two smaller heaters. Apart from providing more even heating, this will prevent the temperature from changing too quickly if one heater fails. If this happens, you should have time to notice and cure the problem before the temperature drops significantly. A heater holder ensures that the heater is not in contact with the substrate, rocks, or aquarium glass. It is also a good idea to use heater guards to prevent fish from resting on the heater and burning themselves or to prevent large, boisterous species from accidentally breaking the heater. A heater guard also helps prevent damage during tank maintenance or when you are moving heavy decor around the tank.

◀ *Always allow the heaterstat to cool down before removing it from the tank. Check the temperature every day using an aquarium thermometer.*

Water management

Tap water is the most convenient source of water for the aquarium, but it is treated to make it fit for human consumption with chemicals that will harm fish. It is therefore essential to condition tap water before you add it to the aquarium—not only when you first fill the tank but also during water changes carried out later on as part of routine maintenance. Used as recommended, liquid tap water conditioners will neutralize chlorine and chloramine and also deal with any heavy metals that the water has picked up on its journey to your home.

◀ *Treating tap water with a conditioner is a simple process. Following the maker's instructions, add the required amount of conditioner to tap water in a bucket before adding it to the tank. Note that not all dechlorinators remove chloramine, so check the label carefully. Ideally, leave the water at room temperature for several hours to take the chill off.*

* Chlorine can also be eliminated by running the water hard into a bucket or by letting it air in a bucket for 24 hours.

MEASURING TANK VOLUME

The length x the width x the depth in inches (centimeters), divided by 231 (1,000), will give you the volume of your aquarium in gallons (liters). However, this calculation does not take into account the displacement of the substrate, equipment, and decor. Filling the aquarium with a bucket of known capacity enables you to measure the volume of water in the aquarium accurately. It is important to know exactly how much water the aquarium holds, because at some future date you may have to treat sick fish with medication diluted according to the volume of the tank. Keep a note of these vital figures.

▲ *Before you start keeping fish, find out what type of water you have, and buy fish that are happy in it. These African Rift Valley Lake cichlids need hard water.*

REVERSE OSMOSIS

◀ Reverse osmosis is a process that removes salts and minerals from the water, plus harmful chemicals and some bacteria, viruses, and fungal spores. For large aquariums (over 6 ft [1.8 m]), investing in a reverse osmosis (R.O.) water purifier (shown left) may be a better long-term option than conditioning tap water each time you need it. However, R.O. water is so pure that you must add minerals back into it to make it suitable for fish keeping.

WATER MANAGEMENT

HOW REVERSE OSMOSIS WORKS

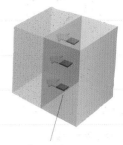

Street pressure forces water through the membrane.

Tap water enters the reverse osmosis unit.

A partially permeable membrane allows only water molecules through.

In normal osmosis, water molecules pass across a partially permeable membrane from a dilute solution to a more concentrated one.

Pure water is drained from the unit.

Leftover water can be used in the garden.

* If buying an R.O. unit does not make economic sense, you can buy supplies of R.O. water from aquatic retailers as you need them.

Water management (continued)

The nitrogen cycle is a biological process that involves the continual circulation of nitrogenous compounds such as ammonia, nitrite, and nitrate. These are the main biological toxins found in the aquarium, so it is important that the nitrogen cycle works effectively to remove these pollutants. The reason for stocking new aquariums slowly is to allow the nitrogen cycle to develop and keep pace with the gradual increase of waste matter. If overfeeding occurs and too many fish are introduced too quickly, the bacteria that form a vital part of the nitrogen cycle will not be sufficiently developed to cope with the influx of waste, and ammonia and nitrites will build up to lethal levels.

THE NITROGEN CYCLE

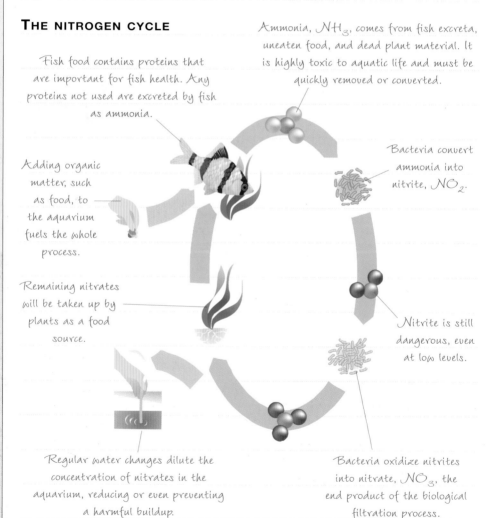

Fish food contains proteins that are important for fish health. Any proteins not used are excreted by fish as ammonia.

Ammonia, NH_3, comes from fish excreta, uneaten food, and dead plant material. It is highly toxic to aquatic life and must be quickly removed or converted.

Adding organic matter, such as food, to the aquarium fuels the whole process.

Bacteria convert ammonia into nitrite, NO_2.

Remaining nitrates will be taken up by plants as a food source.

Nitrite is still dangerous, even at low levels.

Regular water changes dilute the concentration of nitrates in the aquarium, reducing or even preventing a harmful buildup.

Bacteria oxidize nitrites into nitrate, NO_3, the end product of the biological filtration process.

HOW A BIOLOGICAL FILTER MATURES

▼ This graph shows the typical rise and fall
of ammonia, nitrite, and nitrate levels in the
aquarium, assuming a filter start-up product
has been added for the first two weeks.

Green: Ammonia
Pink: Nitrite
Yellow: Nitrate

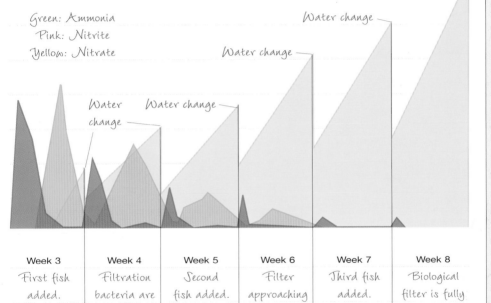

Water change

Water change

Water change

Water
change

Water change

Week 3	Week 4	Week 5	Week 6	Week 7	Week 8
First fish added. Ammonia begins to be produced.	Filtration bacteria are processing waste.	Second fish added. Established bacteria cope with excess ammonia.	Filter approaching maturity.	Third fish added. Filter bacteria adapt to changes.	Biological filter is fully established. Safe to add more sensitive fish.

* A filter start-up product helps the
filter bacteria mature. It can be used
with a new setup and whenever the
biological loading on the filter changes,
such as when new fish are added. See
page 41 for more information on how
to use a start-up product.

▲ The amounts of ammonia,
nitrite, and nitrate peak, one
after the other, as beneficial
bacteria in the biological filter
convert one substance to
the next. The ideal target for
ammonia and nitrite levels is
zero.

Water management (continued)

Controlling the water conditions is the key to a successful aquarium. A vital part of this is to measure, record, and compare the values of a number of characteristics that reflect the state of the water circulating around the tank. The test kits available today are easy to use and provide accurate results. Most involve adding liquid or tablet reagents to a water sample and comparing a color change with a printed chart.

WATER MANAGEMENT

AMMONIA, NITRITE, AND NITRATE

When testing for these substances, it is best to carry out tests for all of them because this will reveal the complete biological status of the aquarium. If you simply test for ammonia and record a zero reading, you may well have a high level of nitrite. Once the first fish have been added, test the water every day until both ammonia and nitrite are under control. Then repeat the tests weekly to ensure that the biological balance of the aquarium is continued. Repeat the tests for a week whenever you add new fish to the aquarium.

◀ This total ammonia test shows a reading of 0.4mg/liter. This toxic short-term level will fall as filter bacteria respond.

◀ A nitrite result of 0.25mg/liter can be fatal for some fish species and must be reduced to zero for safe fish keeping.

If the aquarium appears to be suffering from an algae problem, it is worth testing for phosphate. If allowed to rise above the level at which the aquarium plants can use it as a fertilizer, the excess will become food for fast-growing algae. Always follow the directions when using test kits.

◀ Nitrate levels can go quite high, especially in sparsely planted tanks. This 25mg/liter result is safe for most systems.

The correct pH level of aquarium water depends on the type of fish you intend to keep. The pH level is a measure of how alkaline or acidic the water is. Some fish, such as African Rift Valley Lake cichlids, prefer alkaline, or high pH, conditions. Others, such as discus or dwarf cichlids, prefer acid, or low pH, conditions. The pH level is measured on a scale of 0–14, with 7 being neutral. Anything below 7 is acidic and above 7 is alkaline. Aquarium fish generally live in water with a pH level between 5 and 9.

THE pH SCALE

▶ *The pH scale is logarithmic, meaning that each unit change in pH, say, from 7 to 8, is a times ten change; from 7 to 9 is a times one hundred change, and from 7 to 10 reflects a times one thousand change. This is why sudden changes are stressful to fish.*

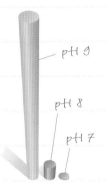

pH 9

pH 8

pH 7

▲ *PH tests are available to provide broad-range (as here) and narrow-range readings. It is a good idea to continue testing pH throughout the life of the aquarium, because ongoing processes such as biological filtration will affect the pH value of the water over time.*

◀ *Dip tests consist of paper or plastic strips with impregnated pads that change color when the strip is dipped briefly in the aquarium water. Here, comparing the color change with the printed chart shows a water hardness of 14°dH.*

WATER HARDNESS

This is a measure of the dissolved mineral salts in the water—the more salts, the harder it is. Total, or general, hardness is made up of temporary and permanent hardness and is measured in degrees of hardness (°dH). Temporary hardness is caused by the presence of calcium bicarbonate in the water and can be removed by boiling. Permanent hardness is caused by calcium and magnesium sulphate and cannot be easily removed.

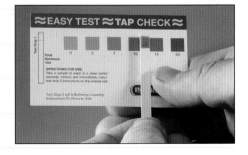

Setting up the tank

On the following pages, we demonstrate the process of setting up a tank measuring 35.5 x 15 x 17.75 in. (90 x 38 x 45 cm). Always allow yourself plenty of time and as few distractions as possible! It is a good idea to have someone to help you assemble and position the tank and stand, since both items are heavy and difficult to maneuver. Make sure you have all the aquarium equipment you will need on hand, plus some essential tools.

Leveling the tank is vital. Even a slight discrepancy will be obvious once you add water.

1 Make sure that both the tank and stand are level in all directions by placing a long spirit (bubble) level along all the edges. If necessary, rest it on a straight wooden batten. Always adjust the cabinet or stand, not the tank.

THE BACKGROUND

At this stage, you should have attached your chosen background to the outside glass (see page 7). In this sequence, we do not fit the background until the later stages so we can more clearly demonstrate the practical sequence of setting up the aquarium.

* *Checklist:*
A long spirit (bubble) level
Screwdriver
Sharp scissors
Water jug
Some old towels
A four-way electrical extension
A plug-in 24-hour timer
Cable ties
2.5-gallon (10-liter) plastic bucket with clear markings to help with measuring water quantities. Keep it solely for aquarium use, and store all your maintenance equipment in it.

2 Wipe the inside of the glass with a clean, ideally new, cloth and water to remove dust; otherwise, it will create a film on the water surface. Never be tempted to use any detergents, as these can be lethal to the fish.

Lay the cable across the base with a 1–1.5 in. (about 3–4 cm) gap between the turns. If there are no suction cups, anchor the cable with handfuls of substrate.

3 Install the heater cable, if used, evenly across the aquarium, guiding it around the rubber suction cups provided. Dampen these to help them stick to the glass base. Keep the cable under slight tension as you feed it around the suction cups.

* Remember to always work from the bottom upward. The first item to go in is the eater cable — see also page 8. Since this will be covered by substrate, it will be impossible to install later on.

see also page 8.

SETTING UP THE TANK

HOW A HEATING CABLE WORKS

A low-wattage cable generates a small amount of extra heat along the lines of the cable. This causes thermal currents in the substrate that move the nutrients around and prevent the substrate from becoming stagnant. This re-creates what happens in nature, where the sun heats the riverbed or lake margin, making the substrate warmer than the water above it. Convection currents create a circulation of water that carries essential nutrients down into the bed.

NUTRIENT FLOW IN NATURE

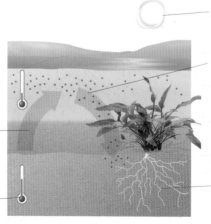

The substrate acts as a "nutrient sink," trapping nutrients where plant roots can easily obtain them.

Water rises by convection as it is warmed by the substrate.

The substrate is slightly warmer than the water above it.

Heat from the sun warms the substrate.

Water circulation carries nutrients down into the substrate.

Plant roots absorb nutrients from the substrate.

Setting up the tank (continued)

Unfortunately, most aquarium substrates, including gravel, do not contain any nutrients and cannot sustain plant growth on their own. The solution is to add a food source to the substrate to ensure healthy plant growth. The most common of these long-term plant food supplements is laterite, a clay-based, reddish additive that provides essential iron to nourish aquarium plants. It needs to be used in conjunction with a bacterial culture that will release the nutrients in a form plants can use.

4 Using a large cup, pour the washed substrate into the aquarium to a depth of about 3 in. (about 7.5 cm), taking care not to disturb the heating cable.

ADDING NUTRIENTS TO THE AQUARIUM

5 Add laterite evenly over the substrate surface, scattering it in a side-to-side pattern.

8 Gently mix the ingredients into the substrate, and smooth out the top.

6 Work methodically from one side of the tank to the other to achieve an even spread.

9 Add a final layer of substrate material to create a finished depth of about 4 in. (10 cm).

7 Add a thin layer of the supplied crumbled bacterial culture on top of the laterite.

The laterite will supply nutrients for several months in the aquarium. After this period, add fertilizer tablets close to the plant roots to continue feeding them.

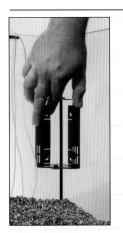

10 Position the filter cradle at one end of the tank, and secure it to the glass using the suction cups supplied. The cradle makes it easy to remove the filter for cleaning at a later date.

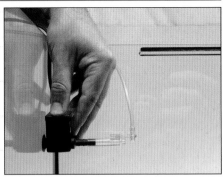

11 Place the filter into the cradle. Turn the filter so the cleaned water flow is directed diagonally across the tank. Leave a gap between the bottom of the filter and the substrate.

13 Place the pump for the pressurized CO_2 system at the opposite end of the tank from the filter, no deeper than 6 in. (15 cm) below the eventual water surface. Any deeper and it would reduce the rate of carbon dioxide diffusion.

▲ *Although the filter and heater are vital pieces of equipment, it is better, from an aesthetic point of view, if they are hidden from view. Plants will conceal them later but leave them accessible.*

12 Using the suction cups supplied, secure the heaterstat to the inside of the back glass. Place it at an angle of 45° so the heat dissipates over a large area. Do not rest it on the substrate.

* Never run the filter pump without water in the tank, as it will burn out. If you want to test it, submerge it in a bucket of water. For the same reason, do not plug in the heater until the tank is full of water.

Setting up the tank (continued)

Now you can begin the creative stage of the setting-up process—positioning the rocks and wood you have cleaned and prepared. In this aquarium, we have chosen two pieces of bogwood that resemble tree roots. If your bogwood looks more like a fallen branch, it might be more effective to lay it down in the tank. Be guided by the shape and graining of the wood, and perhaps experiment with different pieces before making a final decision.

14 Put the bogwood in place, and press it down well to ensure that it does not topple over. If it happens to float, tie the wood with thin nylon fishing line to a stone that you can bury in the substrate.

15 In this setup, there is a piece of wood on each side of the tank. Wood can be used to hide aquarium equipment, but make sure you can still access heaters and filters for routine maintenance.

16 Rocks can be heavy, so lower them carefully to avoid damaging the glass or disturbing the equipment and decor that you have already installed. Make sure they are absolutely stable. Now you can add a few smaller stones and pebbles, if you wish.

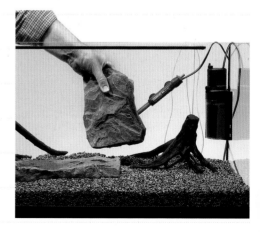

17 Pour the conditioned water carefully from the bucket onto a saucer, a flat stone, or even a plastic bag to prevent the water from splashing and disturbing the substrate too much.

18 This UK model of aquarium is supplied with a tight-fitting surround. It should be installed at this stage in case the water causes the tank to bow slightly at the top when it is full.

Filling the tank to this level minimizes the risk of water overflowing when you introduce the plants.

Adjust the direction and flow rate of the filter if necessary.

19 Continue filling the tank until it is about three-quarters full. The water is bound to look cloudy at first. Now switch on the system. After 12–24 hours, the filter will have cleared the water and the heater will have warmed the water to its preset temperature.

* If you prefer, start filling the tank with a clean glass or plastic jug, and progress to a bucket when the water level has started to rise.

Setting up the tank (continued)

Before putting in any plants, return to your basic plan of the aquarium. Keep the plants in their transportation bags until you are ready to use them so they do not dry out. Start by adding the background plants, and work forward to complete the display. Placing plants in the aquarium takes some practice. If possible, try to work one-handed.

PLANTING TECHNIQUE

◀ *Gently hold the plant near the base and, using a finger of the same hand, make a hole in the substrate. Slide the plant into the hole, just deep enough to prevent it from coming loose.*

◀ *Push the plant carefully into the hole and backfill. The crown should be just above the substrate. Try not to disturb the substrate too much, and work rapidly to keep the hole from filling up.*

20 Working across the back of the tank, put in the first plant. This is one of two *Echinodorus cordifolius* that will occupy the back left-hand corner.

21 The center back is often a key position for a specimen plant. The red and green leaves of *Echinodorus* 'Red Special' will create a fine backdrop.

* Before planting, look at each plant to see if it has a natural front face. Stand back as you work to judge the effect you are creating.

PLANTS AS HIDERS

The right-hand side of the display is dominated by the upright rock, the heaterstat, and the internal filter. Large-leaved plants will disguise the hardware without restricting access to it. Three *Echinodorus* 'Red Flame' are planted in an L shape around the corner of the tank.

* *The advantage of working with one hand becomes clearer as you introduce more plants. The fuller the tank, the more restricted the space you have to work in. Although you must treat the plants gently, place them firmly into the substrate so they do not tilt or fall over.*

MIDGROUND PLANTING

22 Three plants of *Cryptocoryne wendtii* 'Tropica' form a curtain across two-thirds of the midground, leaving the fish with a swimming area toward the left and rear.

A small group of cryptocorynes planted together will develop to form a clump in the midground.

23 Push each plant into the substrate so the roots are in contact with the nutrient layer. Pull in the substrate around the roots to anchor it, as if you were planting it into the ground.

▲ *Take the cryptocoryne from its pot, remove the rockwool, cut away any yellowing leaves, and trim the roots. This plant is ready to go in.*

Setting up the tank (continued)

Complete the planting with some foreground plants. In this display, the left-hand side features *Hygrophila polysperma* 'Rosanervig', a tall plant that will need regular clipping to ensure that it does not take over and block out light to the other foreground plants. In the mid-foreground is *Hemianthus micranthemoides*, a bushy plant with small fine leaves that will also need clipping as they spread. Slightly to the right is *Monosolenium tenerum*, a liverwort that is supplied attached by netting to a rock or specially-made planting stone. And finally, the front right-hand side will be covered by a lush green carpet of *Glossostigma elatinoides*. Together, these plants create an interesting foreground, allowing the fish room to swim, plus cover if they need it.

Hygrophila polysperma 'Rosanervig' — *Echinodorus cordifolius* — *Echinodorus 'Red Special'*

Hemianthus micranthemoides

24 *Hygrophila polysperma* 'Rosanervig' has attractive white veins on the leaves. Regular pruning generates healthy new growth.

25 The foreground display continues with two plants of *Hemianthus micranthemoides* that in time will form a bushy clump up to 6 in. (15 cm) tall.

THE PLANTED AQUARIUM

▼ *As you plant the tank, take a look at it from various angles. If the sides are visible, make sure there is some planting of interest there. This view from the right-hand side of the tank lends a whole new perspective to the work.*

Cryptocoryne wendtii 'Tropica'

Echinodorus 'Red Flame'

Monosolenium tenerum

Glossostigma elatinoides

Cryptocoryne wendtii 'Tropica'

26 In the wild, liverwort *Monosolenium tenerum* forms cushions on stones. Simply place the stone on the substrate. In time, the stone will be completely covered.

27 Given sufficient light, three *Glossostigma elatinoides* will make a dense carpet across the substrate, filling any gaps. Give them room to spread.

Setting up the tank (continued)

The featured U.K. aquarium has a lighting cradle that accepts two fluorescent tubes and fits snugly into the frame over the tank; U.S. tanks have integrated hood-reflector lights. An aquarium may seem brightly lit to our eyes, yet still be too dark for some plants to thrive. Consider the requirements of the plants you choose for your aquarium.

INSTALLING THE LIGHTING SYSTEM

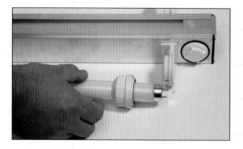 

28 Slip the locking collars onto each tube, and align the pins correctly before sliding them into the sockets at both ends of the lighting cradle.

29 Carefully tighten up the locking collars at each end to secure the tubes in place. These will make a waterproof seal around the endcaps.

The starter (ballast) system for the tubes is housed in the central section of the cradle.

* Always use lighting equipment designed for aquariums. Other sources will not meet the special needs of aquarium plants and may be unsafe for operation close to water.

▲ A view looking down into the aquarium shows the lighting cradle in place, complete with fluorescent tubes. The cradle is part of an aluminum frame that fits over the top of the tank.

USING A FILTER START-UP PRODUCT

Once the tank has reached this stage of the setting-up process, you must allow sufficient time for the filter to mature before introducing any fish. Unfortunately, this can take six to eight weeks—a long time when you want to enjoy the display and stock it with fish. Adding a filter start-up product, available in liquid or powder form, can reduce this time by half or to days. Add one of these products to the system on a regular basis during the first few weeks, beginning as soon as the filter is switched on. Always follow the manufacturer's directions. Monitor what is happening in the filter using aquarium test kits to establish the levels of ammonia, nitrite, and nitrate in the water.

30 Carefully measure the correct amount of filter start-up product needed for your system. Follow the instructions provided with the product exactly.

31 Add the product to the aquarium water. It provides heterotrophic bacteria that will foster the growth of beneficial bacteria to deal with nitrogenous waste.

◀ *Three weeks after the tank was set up, the plants are growing, albeit at different rates. Keep the tank glass clean, and trim back the stems of any plants that have become straggly.*

Adding the fish

Bear in mind that even with the addition of a filter start-up product, you will be introducing your first fish into an environment where very little biological activity is taking place. There is always a chance that the fish will be exposed to less-than-perfect water conditions during the maturation process, so it is important to select species that are known to be hardy. When it comes to buying fish, be sure to buy from a reputable dealer whose advice you can rely on, now and in the future.

HARDY FISH

If a fish is described as hardy, it means that it is able to tolerate changes in water quality during the maturation process; it is not an excuse for allowing the water quality to deteriorate, as any fish will suffer in poor conditions. If anything, you should tend the system with extra care in the early days to ensure that the water quality remains as good as possible for the first fish.

Look for clear eyes.

Check the fins for ragged edges or signs of disease, such as white spots.

▲ A healthy fish will swim in a manner that is typical of the species. The eyes should be clear, neither protuberant nor sunken; the dorsal fin should be erect and all other finnage carried clear of the body, with no serious splits, reddening, or fraying. Missing or raised scales are cause for concern.

▲ Look carefully at all the fish in a dealer's tank before buying. Never buy a fish on impulse; first ensure that you are not taking on something that will cause you or its tankmates problems in the future. Do your research!

* Remember that your first fish will form part of the finished display, and you need to consider how they will coexist with the species you add later on.

ADVICE ON BUYING FISH

- If possible, buy fish from a dealer in your locality. His water chemistry is likely to be close to your own, so the fish for sale will adapt readily to your own (conditioned) tap water.
- It is likely that the fish for sale will be juveniles. Make due allowance for growth, and base your stocking levels on the size your fish are likely to attain. Find out their maximum adult size.
- Visit dealers at fairly quiet times, when they can give you more attention. It is in the dealer's interest to look after customers, whatever their level of knowledge.
- To be certain of buying or ordering the right fish, quote the scientific, not the common, name. *Zebra fish* can apply to cichlids, danios, or catfish.
- The colors of fish for sale may appear muted. Some attain full color as they mature; others will show better colors in a home aquarium with a darkish substrate and refuges.
- It is reasonable to specify individual fish if you want a pair or if some are larger or a better color than others of the same species, but do not expect staff to net, say, individual neon tetras.

BAGGING UP THE FISH

1 Once the dealer has placed your fish in a plastic bag, take the opportunity to view them from below to check that they are healthy.

2 When you are satisfied, the dealer will tie a tight knot in the top of the bag, trapping air and water for the journey home.

3 To prevent fish from becoming trapped in the corners, this dealer slides the upturned bag into a second bag, tucking in the corners.

4 The dealer then places both bags with care instructions into a plastic or paper bag so the fish travel in the dark to reduce stress.

Adding the fish (continued)

Go straight home after buying your fish so they spend the least possible time in transit and are therefore subject to less stress. Turn off the tank lights before floating the bags with the fish inside in the tank. Some fishkeepers will not tip transit water into their aquarium because it is ammonia laden. However, unless you are unloading several large bags into a small tank, dilution and filtration will take care of any pollutants. The main concern is not to stress the fish, which you will do if you lift the fish out of their bags.

INTRODUCING THE FISH

▶ Following a short journey home, float the unopened bags in the aquarium for about 20 minutes to allow the water temperatures to equalize before releasing the fish.

▲ After a long journey, first roll down the sides of the bag to allow stale air to escape. Then leave the bags to float in the tank for about 20 minutes to equalize the water temperatures.

▶ To release the fish, hold the bag just below the water surface, tipping it slightly to encourage the fish to swim out. Make sure you have released them all. Repeat the process with each bag. Some fish are timid and may hide at first, but this is quite natural.

▶ After two weeks or so, when your first fish have
been safely introduced and are thriving in the
aquarium, you can think about adding
more fish, such as this Odessa
barb. Try to choose fish that
will add interest to the tank at
all levels—bottom, midwater, and
surface—and that will coexist peacefully.
If in doubt, ask your aquarium dealer for advice.

ADDING THE FISH

QUARANTINING FISH

You should always quarantine new
purchases before adding them to an
existing community. The tank need
only be basic, with a heaterstat, an
air-driven sponge filter, and a refuge
for the fish. A week or two in isolation
is good insurance against introducing
stress-related diseases, such as
white spot, to your aquarium. And if a
new fish does become sick, it can be
medicated in situ, avoiding possible
side effects to existing stock.

* A quarantine tank has many
other uses. It is a place to house the
occasional sick, bullied, or harassed
fish; baby fish; or any tank
inhabitants that cannot tolerate
treatments being used in the main
tank. It can be small — 17.75 ×
9.75 × 9.75 in. (45 × 25 × 25
cm)—and can be stored dry when
not in use. Keep a separate net and
other equipment for the quarantine
tank to avoid cross contamination.

A QUARANTINE TANK

Include an item of decor to
provide refuge for the fish.

A simple
internal sponge
filter sustains a
useful population
of beneficial
bacteria.

A heaterstat
maintains water
temperature at
the same level as
that in the main
display tank.

An air pump
powers the
sponge filter.

A shallow bed
of clean gravel
can be used, but
a bare bottom
is preferable.

Feeding fish

Aquarium fish need a regular balanced diet if they are to thrive, and they depend totally on the fish keeper to provide it. Good-quality, manufactured dried foods will supply all the fish's requirements, but you can supplement these with once-live foods in a freeze-dried or frozen form. To delay deterioration, store tubs of flake food in a cool, dry place—never on top of the tank hood—and replace the lid immediately after every feed.

DRIED FOODS

Sinking granules suit bottom— feeding species.

Tablet foods resemble flake foods, but in a different form.

Flake foods are ideal for small to medium-size fish.

Algae wafers suit herbivorous algae eaters and bottom-feeding catfish.

◀ Food tablets stuck onto the glass gradually disintegrate, attracting fish from all parts of the aquarium.

FROZEN FOOD

Frozen food is available in convenient blister packs.

FREEZE-DRIED FOODS

Freeze-dried mosquito larvae can form part of a varied diet.

A defrosted cube of bloodworms makes a treat. Do not refreeze.

Freeze-dried tubifex is a safe way of offering this excellent food.

* Ideally, offer freeze-dried and frozen foods to your fish as a treat, in conjunction with a flake food diet. This gives the fish variations in food texture and the most complete diet.

LIVE FOODS

▼ *Adding a batch of bloodworms to the aquarium prompts an immediate feeding response from the fish. This is a good opportunity to observe them at close quarters. Use feeding times to check that all the fish are present and to make sure they are all getting a fair share of the food.*

▲ *Suitable live foods include daphnia (left), bloodworms (center), and brine shrimp (right). They are supplied in plastic bags full of water. Strain the foods through a fine net. Do not put the water in the tank.*

◀ *Secure lettuce leaves in a clip so that herbivorous fish can graze on them. The fish usually ignore lettuce that's left to float.*

VACATION FEEDING

Healthy adult fish can happily go without feeding for a week or so. If you are away for longer, package up daily rations of flake or freeze-dried food in a twist of foil for a sitter to administer. Vacation feeding blocks are another option.

▶ *Small sticks gradually release food over a weekend. Larger vacation feeding blocks last for a week.*

HOW MUCH TO FEED

Overfeeding is the most common cause of water quality problems, which in turn lead to fish health issues. The golden rule is to offer a little at a time. With flake foods, start by offering a small pinch, say half a dozen flakes. If the fish eat them all within five minutes, add a little more. Remove any uneaten food with a net. Feed fish once a day for the first two months after setting up the aquarium. This allows the biological system to establish without placing an excessive strain on the filtration bacteria. Thereafter, you can feed the fish twice daily.

* Always check that no one else in the household has fed the fish before you do.

Health care

Learn what is normal behavior for your various fish so that if they deviate from it, you will have an early warning that something may be wrong. Your eyes are the best diagnostic tools at your disposal, and with practice and experience you can detect early signs of water quality, compatibility, and disease problems before they become acute.

PHYSICAL SIGNS

Look out for unusually pale or dark colors; the development of spots, ulcers, or white patches; frayed or reddish fins; cloudy or bulging eyes; slimy or bloodshot skin; raised scales; and a thin, swollen, or asymmetrical belly. Feeding is a good time to check for problems.

▲ *White spot is a widespread fish disease, and as it usually comes in with new stock, quarantine is still the most effective way to tackle it. Pinhead-size white dots appear on the skin and fins, and severely affected fish may gasp because of irritation of the gills. Any species can become infected. Treat it as soon as possible with an over-the-counter remedy.*

▼ *For demonstration only, the fish featured here has symptoms of all the common ailments that tropical freshwater fish may suffer from in the aquarium. Most are easy to identify and treat.*

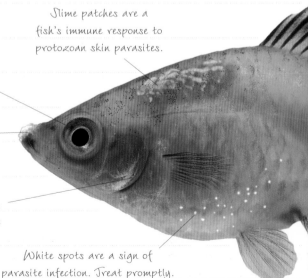

Slime patches are a
fish's immune response to
protozoan skin parasites.

Swollen eyes can be seen in
fish with dropsy.
A tumor behind the eye
could also cause swelling.

Mouth rot could
be a bacterial or
a fungal infection.

Rapid gill movements could
be the result of water quality
problems, as well as parasites
or bacterial infection.

White spots are a sign of
parasite infection. Treat promptly.

PREPARING MEDICATIONS

1 Calculate the correct amount of medication for your tank, and add the solution to a plastic container of water taken from the aquarium.

2 Thoroughly mix the medication into the water. By diluting it, you avoid producing localized spots of dangerously high concentrations.

3 Gently introduce the diluted medication into the aquarium. Remember to keep any utensils solely for aquarium use. Follow the maker's directions.

HEALTH CARE

If you experience a mysterious health problem, it may not be a disease. Check all the water quality values, then do a partial water change to see if that improves things. Check that all equipment is functioning normally, and consider whether anything poisonous (medications, inappropriate decor) could have been added to the aquarium. And ask yourself if the problem could be the result of breeding behavior or bullying.

Fine gold spots may be velvet disease.

Fungus is treated with medication.

Ragged fins with redness may be bacterial fin rot.

* Regular maintenance, keeping the substrate clean, and reducing stress help keep fish healthy.

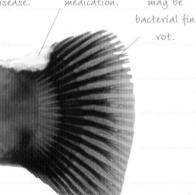

Protruding scales are a symptom of dropsy. Use an internal bacterial treatment.

BEHAVIORAL SIGNS

Common behavioral signs of distress are hiding, refusing to feed, resting on the surface or the bottom, breathing heavily, holding fins clamped, darting around the aquarium, and swimming with irregular movements or in odd positions. However, remember that some of these activities are normal for certain species.

Regular maintenance

A display aquarium is a living environment that will change and develop over a period of time. To keep the fish and plants healthy and looking good, it is essential to carry out a program of routine maintenance. This should not be too time consuming; look at it as an opportunity to observe and enjoy your aquarium in action.

WATER CHANGES

The purpose of making a water change is to reduce the nitrates that can build up in the tank. This is also a good opportunity for removing algae and debris from the substrate, using a self-priming, siphon-action gravel cleaner.

Siphon water out of the tank, making sure you do not trap any fish. A flexible hose attached to the siphon takes water from the aquarium.

◀ Guide the foot of the gravel cleaner gently over the plant leaves to remove any fine, dead algae growth.

◀ Move the cleaner over the substrate, going from one side of the tank to the other to collect organic debris.

* Do not remove more than a total of 25% of the aquarium water. As the bucket fills up, stop siphoning and empty the bucket. Keep the last bucket of water to clean the filter.

SAFETY FIRST

Before carrying out any work on the tank, turn off the electricity supply and unplug it, just in case someone switches it back on by mistake.

▲ Direct the water from the tank into a bucket on the ground.

CLEANING THE FILTER

1 Working over the bucket of water removed from the tank, remove the impeller and put it in the water.

2 Remove the filter foam from the casing. Using tank water means you will not destroy the beneficial bacteria in the foam.

3 Wipe out the casing with filter wool dipped in aquarium water. Remove any plant fragments from the slots in the lid.

4 Clean off any slime on the impeller and the shaft. Clean the insert plate that holds the filter media in place.

5 Clean the foam by squeezing it out in the tank water. Replace half of it (see below) when it no longer returns to its original shape.

6 Reassemble the filter in the reverse order of dismantling it. Replace it in the tank, ensuring that it floods fully.

RENEWING THE FOAM

When renewing filter foam—every 6–12 months—cut the old and new pieces in half. Run the new and old halves together for a month to allow the new filter foam to become seeded with the nitrifying bacteria.

* Replace the filter foam carefully in the casing so water cannot bypass it, making the filter inefficient. Do not allow the foam to dry out during cleaning. Return the unit to the tank as soon as possible.

REGULAR MAINTENANCE

Regular maintenance (continued)

You will need to carry out some maintenance tasks every day, others every one to two weeks, some monthly, and others less frequently. These time lines are only a guide, as each tank will vary depending on its size, method of filtration, and the number of fish you keep. By noting all your actions in an aquarium log, you will soon see a pattern developing that is right for your tank. Should a problem arise, you can refer back to see what has changed, and you might have an answer to your problem.

EVERY DAY

- Check the water temperature
- Check for missing fish and any signs of ill health or distress
- Check that the equipment is operating properly (filter, lights, air pumps, etc.)
- Feed the fish and remove any uneaten food

▼ *Among the routine maintenance tasks that you need to carry out every 7–14 days, the most important ones are geared toward keeping the water in good condition, such as regular water changes and tests for toxic waste products. Test the water for pH, ammonia, nitrite, and nitrate levels.*

EVERY 7–14 DAYS

▲ *Clean the front of the glass to prevent the buildup of algae. Use a pad of filter wool, an algae magnet, or an algae scraper on the end of a handle (above right).*

▲ *Following a water change and gravel cleaning, refill the tank with conditioned water at the same temperature as that in the display aquarium.*

◀ *Clean the filter in aquarium water every 4 to 6 weeks. See the sequence on page 51.*

PLANT MAINTENANCE

Keeping the aquarium plants growing well and looking their best is one of the long-term objectives of routine maintenance.

▲ *To encourage a bushy habit in plants such as* Hemianthus, *trim away excess growth with sharp scissors. One thorough "haircut" is better than snipping away piecemeal every few days.*

* Remove the trimmings of bushy plants with a fine net when you have finished cutting.

◀ *Feed plants with liquid fertilizer, following the manufacturer's directions, and replenish tablet fertilizers as required.*

EVERY 6–12 MONTHS

- Replace half the filter foam
- Replace the filter pump impeller
- Check that the quarantine/hospital tank filter is working properly

◀ *If one plant is taking over or generally spreading beyond its allocated growing space, do not be afraid to trim it back. Cut it just above a node so the plant produces new bushy growth.*

DEALING WITH ALGAE

High phosphate and nitrate levels plus excess light can boost algae growth. Phosphate is present in tap water and is also gradually added to the aquarium via fish food. If you suspect that it is causing a problem, carry out a water test and take appropriate action. This includes reducing the lighting and increasing the rate of small (10%) partial water changes, using water containing less phosphate. A chemical resin filter medium will rapidly reduce the level.

REGULAR MAINTENANCE

FISH, PLANTS, AND THEMED AQUARIUMS

This part of the book presents a selection of popular freshwater fish and aquarium plants plus a look at some ideas for setting up aquariums that reflect natural habitats around the world.

To make sense of the wide range of freshwater fish available at your local dealer, it helps to consider them in their families or groups. Members of one family will share some common characteristics, such as body shape and lifestyle preferences. There are exceptions, of course, but this way you will begin to recognize species from each family or group and can set up the right conditions for them in your aquarium. The groups featured in this section are cichlids, catfish, barbs, characins, anabantoids, danios and rasboras, rainbowfish, livebearers, and loaches and sharks.

As we have seen on pages 36–39, aquarium plants form an important visual element of a successful display. They also perform useful functions within the aquarium, such as helping keep the water fresh and providing shelter for nervous fish. And floating plants in particular are often vital to encourage certain fish to spawn. The plants featured on pages 74–83 are arranged in A–Z order of their

▶ *Fish such as the royal panaque (above) and ram (above right) would suit this aquarium well.*

scientific names and in such a way that you can clearly see approximately how big they become and whether they are rooted or free floating.

The last section of the book showcases a number of biotope aquariums that simulate environments as varied as cool fast-flowing streams to warm freshwater swamps. Setting these up is a test of your design skills your well as your knowledge of

the plants and decor that echo the real habitat. Add the right fish, and you have begun a new adventure in creative fish keeping.

CICHLIDS

Cichlids

The cichlids are an extremely diverse family, ranging in size from less than an inch (a couple of centimeters) to three feet (almost a meter) long, with considerable variations in shape and coloration. They are noted for their dietary specializations—if something edible exists, a cichlid will have evolved to exploit it. Despite this variability, cichlids all look after their eggs and young. Some lay their eggs on a surface and guard them and the resulting fry; others protect the eggs or larvae in the mouth(s) of one or both parents, usually the mother. This behavior is fascinating but does have a downside—defending the brood often means attacking other fish in the aquarium. Cichlids are found throughout the tropics in the Americas and Africa, plus three species in Asia.

◀ *The cockatoo dwarf cichlid (Apistogramma cacatuoides) is small, beautiful, and peaceful—the ideal combination. As a bonus, it displays fascinating breeding behavior. Here, a highly colorful male escorts a female toward a plastic tube "cave."*

▶ *The ram, or butterfly dwarf cichlid* (Mikrogeophagus ramirezi), *is justifiably popular for its color and gentle disposition. It is fine for a general community aquarium with soft, slightly acid water.*

The male ram has dazzling colors.

The female has a mauve-pink area on the lower flank.

A brown discus, a typical wild type from which aquarium forms have been bred

One of many color forms

◀ *The discus (Symphysodon aequifasciatus) is a very distinctive fish from the Amazon River. Breeding has produced a wide range of color variants very different from the wild fish. These fish are best kept in shoals. The young fry feed from secretions on the parents' flanks.*

▼ The fairy cichlid (Neolamprologus brichardi) *is one of the easiest, most readily available, and behaviorally most interesting of the dwarf cichlids from Lake Tanganyika in East Africa. These fish reach up to 2.75 in. (7 cm) in length.*

▶ *The angel (Pterophyllum scalare) is perhaps the most widely kept of all cichlids, although not a typical cichlid shape. Color forms in the hobby include koi (right) and marbled varieties.*

Normal form

Daffodil variety

This is a wild-caught angel with attractive lace finnage.

▶ *Kribs (Pelvicachromis pulcher) are the nearest thing to the ideal beginner's cichlid— small, colorful, fairly peaceful, and easy to keep and breed. The males grow up to 3 in. (about 8 cm) in length; the females to about 2.5 in. (6.5 cm). These fascinating fish are native to the coastal lowlands of Nigeria.*

Male—with tail spot and pointed pelvic fins

Female—deeper bodied

Female—distinctive in color from the male, depending on variety

▶ *Many of the rock-dwelling cichlids that live in Lake Malawi are available for hobbyists to enjoy. These fish are known locally as mbuna. One of the easiest is Trewavas's mbuna (Labeotropheus trewavasae).*

Male—here showing the droop nose seen in both sexes

Catfish

Grouping catfish into one category is difficult, as there are many hundreds of species, but the most common groups kept in aquariums are the *Corydoras* and *Synodontis* species. Given their small size, peaceful nature, and useful feeding habits, it is not surprising that the corydoras group of catfish are some of the most popular fish kept in the hobby. Although not particularly demanding in the aquarium, they are in constant contact with the substrate and therefore vulnerable to bacterial infections, so be sure to keep the substrate clean. Synodontis catfish are also scavengers, but unlike the corydoras, they can reach a formidable size and are best suited to a community of larger fish. The selection of catfish shown here also reflects their fascinating diversity.

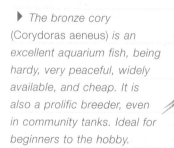

▶ *The bristlenose catfish* (Ancistrus *sp.*) *is well named for the soft outgrowths ("bristles") on the heads of both sexes, which are longer and more branched on males* (right). *These peaceful fish from northern Brazil will help keep the tank free of algae.*

This is the leucistic, semi-albino, form.

▶ *The bronze cory* (Corydoras aeneus) *is an excellent aquarium fish, being hardy, very peaceful, widely available, and cheap. It is also a prolific breeder, even in community tanks. Ideal for beginners to the hobby.*

There is also a true albino form, a human-bred long-finned variety, and a black variant that may prove to be a separate species.

◀ *The attractive Sterba's cory* (Corydoras sterbai) *enjoys warm conditions and will thrive in a community aquarium kept at 77-86°F (25-30°C). It is best kept in groups of six, with two males for every female.*

▶ In the wild, the upside-down catfish (Synodontis nigriventris) spends much of its time in an inverted position, picking mosquito larvae from the surface or beneath leaves. In the aquarium, it is peaceful and good-natured, if a little shy.

◀ Many catfish eat algae, and by doing so, help keep an aquarium clean. Among the smaller algae eaters is otocinclus (Otocinclus sp.), most reaching only 1.5 in. (4 cm) long. These fish will settle in any size aquarium and busily clear away any algae.

▼ Twig catfish (Farlowella sp.) are well named for their shape and color, which help them avoid predation in their South American home. They reach about 6 in. (15 cm) long and appreciate a quiet spot.

▲ In the glass catfish (Kryptopterus bicirrhis), the backbone and internal organs are clearly visible. This delicate fish grows to 4 in. (10 cm) and likes areas of vegetation in which to hide. Always keep glass catfish in a small shoal.

The snout is broader in males and bears bristles.

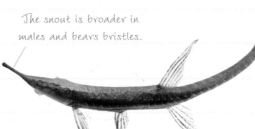

Barbs

The name *barb*, meaning "beard," derives from the whiskerlike barbels in the corner of the mouth; but whereas some species have one or two pairs of these sensory appendages, others lack them. Their relatively small size makes them vulnerable to predation, but they are equipped with excellent vision and ability to sprint to avoid capture. In the aquarium, these resourceful, active shoalers accept a wide range of small foods, and many will spawn, scattering hundreds of adhesive or semiadhesive eggs in plants or over the substrate after a brief, vigorous courtship.

◀ *The rosy barb* (Puntius conchonius) *is so called because of the reddish tinge that suffuses the silvery flanks, which intensifies when pairs are ready to spawn. The copper rosy barb is a farmed variant with elongated finnage and a gold-edged black spot in front of the tail. Both the rosy and copper rosy barbs grow to a length of 6 in. (15 cm).*

Copper rosy barb

▶ *With its black vertical bars along the body and its rosy glow, the black ruby barb* (Puntius nigrofasciatus) *makes an excellent alternative to the more demanding tiger barb. The black ruby barb from Sri Lanka achieves a maximum adult size of 2.5 in. (6.5 cm) and prefers to be kept in a small shoal in an aquarium with some plant growth for shade from bright lighting.*

Female

Male-in front

▶ *The fiveband barb* (Puntius pentazona) *always seems interested in its surroundings and constantly roams the aquarium in search of food. Provide a varied diet. This hardy fish grows to 2 in. (5 cm) and does best when kept in a small shoal.*

◀ *Tiger barbs* (Puntius tetrazona) *are very active shoaling fish with a defined hierarchy within the shoal. Be sure to keep them in a group of at least six individuals. They have a reputation for fin nipping, so do not house them with long-finned species or slow swimmers, such as Siamese fighting fish or angelfish.*

▶ *At 2 in. (5 cm), the cherry barb* (Puntius titteya) *is one of the smallest barbs but makes up for its lack of size with stunning red body coloration. To keep the color bright, include some flake food containing spirulina algae. These peaceful fish do well in a group of five or six and suit any community display.*

A male showing typical bright red color

Note the tiny barbels near the mouth.

Characers

The characers are one of the largest groups of fish available in the aquarium hobby and include the popular tetras. Characers have an adaptation known as the Weberian apparatus, which connects the hearing organs and the swim bladder, allowing the swim bladder to amplify sounds and provide the fish with an enhanced sense of hearing. Other senses are also more acute in many of the characers, and the fish are very aware of changes in their environment. This makes them particularly good at forming shoals, finding food, and escaping danger. In the aquarium, take care that vibrations or other stress factors do not shock the fish.

▶ *The black widow tetra (Gymnocorymbus ternetzi) comes from South America. It tolerates one of the widest ranges of pH of any aquarium fish, so it will do well in almost any setup. It grows to a maximum of 2 in. (5 cm).*

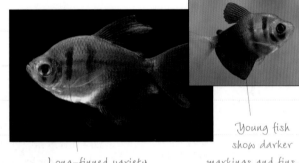

Young fish show darker markings and fins.

Long-finned variety

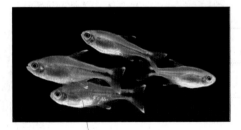

Males are more colorful than females.

◀ *Despite reaching only 2 in. (5 cm), the silver-tip tetra (Hasemania nana) is a striking, streamlined fish that will enjoy swimming in the outlet flow from a power filter. Keep it in a group of six, and provide plenty of swimming space as well as plant cover to help the fish feel secure.*

▶ *The stunning emperor tetra (Nematobrycon palmeri) from Colombia adds a touch of purple to an aquarium display. It has a placid nature, so do not house this 2-in. (5-cm) species with large, boisterous tankmates. In the right conditions, the emperor tetra is a long-lived fish.*

Female

Male

▶ *In the cardinal tetra (Paracheirodon axelrodi), the red band runs the entire length of the body. To see these midwater swimmers at their best, keep them in a large shoal of 25 to 30 fish or even more. This way, they will exhibit the natural shoaling behavior seen in their native Brazilian habitat.*

The cardinal tetra requires soft, slightly acidic water conditions. Do not introduce it into a newly set-up aquarium.

◀ *The beautiful little neon tetra (Paracheirodon innesi) from Peru grows to 1.5 in. (4 cm) and is probably one of the best-known aquarium fish. Neons require good water conditions and similar-size tankmates—larger species might regard them as an easy meal. In a group of at least six individuals, they will demonstrate their natural shoaling behavior and bring the aquarium to life with vibrant color.*

The male Congo tetra has long flowing fins.

▶ *Being one of the largest popular tetras at 3.25 in. (8.5 cm), the Congo tetra (Phenacogrammus interruptus) needs plenty of swimming space. But it is a timid species and will not thrive with boisterous fish.*

Anabantoids

Anabantoids are perhaps the most diverse and varied of all freshwater fish. They include the bubblenesting bettas and gouramis from Southeast Asia, mouthbrooding species from the same area, and free-spawning species from Africa. They all possess an auxiliary breathing organ, in addition to their gills, called the labyrinth organ, which allows them to breathe atmospheric air at the water surface. Without access to the surface, they could drown!

◀ ▲ *Do not house the Siamese fighting fish* (Betta splendens) *with species that might be tempted to nip at the male's wonderful flowing fins, seen in shades of red, blue, green, or gold. Never keep more than one male per tank, as they will fight to the death. However, it is safe to house a male-female pair or one male to two females. Provide plant cover in which the female can find refuge if she is not ready to breed. The fish grow to a maximum size of 2.75 in. (7 cm).*

▶ *The dwarf gourami* (Colisa lalia) *from India and Borneo grows to 2 in. (5 cm) and is a favorite choice for the small- to medium-size community aquarium. The color variants are many, but the most popular are those with the natural diagonal red-and-cobalt blue stripes. Keep these fish in pairs (females have less vibrant colors) with quiet tankmates in a well-planted tank.*

▶ *The paradise fish (Macropodus opercularis)
is a robust species whose only drawback is its
aggression toward its own and other species. At
3.5 in. (9 cm), males are slightly larger and more
colorful than females, which
also lack the male's flowing
fins. The paradise fish is said
to be the first-ever ornamental
tropical freshwater species
kept as a pet in Europe. It
originated in Southeast Asia.*

Orange male

Silver male

*Males have
extended, almost
pointed dorsal
fins.*

◀ *As long as it is housed with other
peaceful species, the pearl gourami
(Trichogaster leeri) can be quite long
lived for an aquarium species, surviving
up to eight years. Its stunning coloration
and elaborate fins explain its popularity.
Pearl gouramis are usually sold in pairs
and occupy the upper layers of a
planted tank. Both sexes grow to
4.75 in. (12 cm).*

*The flanks are
spotted.*

*As it matures,
the male develops
a red breast.*

*The markings of the three-spot
gourami provide camouflage.*

▶ *The three-spot
(opaline) gourami
(Trichogaster
trichopterus) is named
for the two black body
markings, the third "spot"
being the eye. Being a
slow-moving species, it
may be targeted by more
active fish, so choose its
tankmates with care.*

Danios and rasboras

Most danios and rasboras are excellent community fish and good starter choices for new aquariums or new fish keepers. They are generally peaceful and have an active, shoaling nature, although some can be quite timid. Some require well-filtered, oxygenated water, wheareas others are less demanding. Open swimming spaces are important, plus planted areas for cover and retreat. Most are relatively small, although some can grow to reasonable sizes, so make sure your aquarium is large enough to accommodate them when fully grown.

▶ *The pearl danio* (Danio albolineatus) *is ideal for the community aquarium, but make sure it has a tight cover, as this fish likes to jump. At 2 in. (5 cm), males are slightly smaller than females but more brightly colored. Keep at least five of these shoaling fish together in a tank with plenty of swimming space.*

This is the elegant long-finned form of the zebra danio.

◀ *The zebra danio* (Danio rerio) *is a very lively but peaceful fish that swims at all levels and prefers a well-planted aquarium with open swimming areas. A few color morphs are available, including the leopard danio, although whether it is a separate species or a variation is not clear. Both zebra and leopard danios are ideal for a small community display. They thrive on a diet that includes some small frozen or live foods.*

▶ With their unique tail pattern and their silver, black, and white coloration, plus their swimming action, a shoal of scissortail rasboras (Rasbora trilineata) will resemble pairs of scissors swimming through the water. The fish rarely grow to more than 3 in. (about 8 cm), so do not keep them with boisterous barbs.

The tail markings are distinctive.

Male (normal form)

◀ With a maximum adult size of 1.5 in. (4 cm), the agile little White Cloud Mountain minnow (Tanichthys albonubes) makes a peaceful addition to any aquarium. The red-and-white fins contrast well with the body coloration and the white stripe running along the flanks. They will show their best colors if fed on live foods. Originally from China, White Cloud Mountain minnows appreciate a cool aquarium (no more than 71.6°F [22°C]) with strong but not turbulent filtration and dense cover from fine-leaved plants. They are among the most commonly kept first community fish. Keep them in groups of at least six, as lone fish become timid and lose their color.

Female (normal form)

Golden form

▶ The harlequin rasbora (Trigonostigma heteromorpha) from Southeast Asia has a distinctive black triangle on the rear of the body and shows its best colors when kept in a group of at least six individuals. Females are deeper bodied, with a straight front edge to the black marking. These lively fish prefer to swim in the upper half of the aquarium and appreciate the cover provided by floating plants.

RAINBOWFISH

Rainbowfish

With their bright colors and peaceful disposition, rainbowfish make ideal aquarium subjects, and many are easy to breed. In the aquarium, these active top-and midwater swimmers are adaptable to a range of water conditions, as long as their environment is well filtered and regularly maintained. Provide areas of open swimming space. Most rainbowfish do not develop their full coloration until they are mature, usually at about 12 months of age, so do not make the mistake of overlooking them in dealers' tanks.

▶ *Threadfin rainbowfish (Iriatherina werneri) from Northern Australia and western New Guinea look delicate but are hardy in soft, slightly acidic water. Keep them in groups of five or more with other calm fish or in a tank of their own. Males have fin extensions, used for display.*

This is a male of the New Guinea red form. Australian forms are more yellow.

▶ *Boeseman's rainbowfish (Melanotaenia boesemani) is a very popular species that shows its best colors when mature (right). The males have the bright orange color and a deeper body than females do. Keep at least one pair in a community aquarium, or give them a tank of their own for a splendid display.*

These young fish are just showing color. Males will grow to about 4 in. (10 cm).

RAINBOWFISH

◀ The iridescent blue body and red fins show this to be a male dwarf neon rainbowfish (Melanotaenia praecox). Females have red-orange fins and a silver body. At only 2 in. (5 cm) long, these are superb rainbowfish for a compact community aquarium, where they will live happily in a group of at least five.

▶ At up to 4.75 in. (12 cm) long, the banded rainbowfish (Melanotaenia trifasciata) is one of the larger rainbowfish and the easiest to breed. Ideally, keep it in a group of three males to two females. It's a lively and colorful community fish.

FORKTAIL RAINBOWFISH

This elegant fish (Pseudomugil furcatus) from Eastern New Guinea will thrive in a small shoal kept with threadfin rainbowfish. All the members of this group are petite, reaching about 2 in. (5 cm) long, and are known as blue eyes. The male (shown here) is more showy and has a longer first dorsal fin than the female has.

▶ Red rainbowfish (Glossolepis incisus) are distinctive for their bold color and sturdy shape—especially in mature males, which become deep bodied as they mature and more intense in color in the presence of females. These are peaceful, adaptable fish.

A mature male at 4.75 in. (12 cm) long

Livebearers

Livebearers are a hardy group of fish, ideal for the beginner aquarist. They include guppies, mollies, platies, and swordtails, all available in a huge diversity of colors and fin shapes. However, true breeding strains are difficult to maintain. Selective breeding is essential, as these cultivated fish will always revert to the wild form. After a gestation period, the female gives birth to fully formed young fish. At birth, these tiny replicas of their parents lack only their color and mature finnage.

▼ *A male flashes its vibrant tail fin.*

▶ *A subtle blue color form*

From its origins in Venezuela and the Caribbean islands, including Barbados, the guppy (Poecilia reticulata) has been spread around the globe for two major reasons: for mosquito larvae control, its preferred food, and within the fish-keeping hobby, for which it has been bred into countless fancy varieties. It is a hugely popular aquarium fish, being cheap and rewarding to keep. It breeds readily.

◀ *A mosaic or leopard body pattern*

▲ *Female (top) and male below*

▶ *The sailfin molly* (Poecilia velifera), *originally from Mexico, is an elegant species in which the male's magnificent dorsal fin and vibrant markings contrast with the more muted colors of the female, as shown here in a pair of green sailfin mollies. A lyretail form (right) shows up well against black.*

◀ *The black molly* (Poecilia sphenops) *has an understated beauty, ideally velvety black all over. These fish thrive in medium-hard water and will feed greedily at the surface. Young born in a planted tank will grow rapidly in the right conditions.*

▶ *The male swordtail* (Xiphophorus helleri) *has the tail extension and the usual rodlike gonopodium formed from the rays of the anal fin. This is used to inseminate the females.*

▶ *The platy* (Xiphophorus maculatus) *is the ideal starter fish for beginners to the hobby. It is easy to keep and feed and will mix well with other community fish. Color forms range from bright red wagtails to more reserved patterns such as the mainly black "tuxedo" form shown above (often with a blue glint to the scales). The more slender variatus* (X. variatus) *has been bred into many showy fin and color forms, including hi-fins.*

This is a male sunset hi-fin variatus.

LIVEBEARERS

Loaches and sharks

Loaches are well known for their active, playful nature and unusual habits. In particular, some loaches rest on their sides or in odd positions, but this is no cause for concern. Loaches have no scales, which gives them a sleek appearance but also makes them more sensitive to chemicals and treatments. Since loaches are scavengers, be sure to provide a smooth substrate that will not damage their barbels. Within the "sharks," some fish are closely related whereas others are not, but all share the streamlined body shape and bold dorsal fin from which they get their common name.

◀ *The svelte tricolor shark (Balantiocheilus melanopterus) justifies its common name, with a tall dorsal fin and a predatory look. In fact, it is a placid fish for a spacious community tank.*

▶ *The dwarf chain loach (Yasuhikotakia sidthimunki) is a beautifully marked, active little fish that will dash about the aquarium and live happily with other energetic fish.*

◀ *Constantly on the move, zebra loaches (Botia striata) will explore and investigate all the surfaces within the aquarium, using their sensitive barbels to locate scraps of food. Keep these sociable fish in groups, and they will reward you with hours of activity. They will reach 4 in. (10 cm).*

▼ *Built on the same body plan, the clown loach* (Chromobotia macracanthus) *has a striking color pattern and a more sociable nature. Keep it in groups of five or more in a community of robust fish.*

▲ *The red-tailed black shark* (Epalzeorhynchos bicolor) *is a truly distinctive fish with bold, simple markings. It is best kept alone because of its belligerent tendencies.*

▲ *The rainbow shark* (Epalzeorhynchos frenatum) *is a slimmer fish that will get along with most hardy tankmates but can squabble occasionally. Feed it well and don't buy malnourished specimens.*

▲ *The Siamese algae eater* (Crossocheilus siamensis) *earns its keep in a community aquarium by eating many nuisance forms of algae. Keep it singly or in groups, and do give it vegetables and other foods.*

◀ *The kuhli loach* (Pangio kuhlii) *is adept at hiding away most of the time, except when food is offered. It will grow to 4.75 in. (12 cm) long and scavenge in the substrate.*

Aquarium plants

The choice of aquatic plants is extensive, with an array of shapes and sizes every bit as diverse as in terrestrial plants. Faced with such a choice, your first consideration must be the size of the aquarium and the type of display you wish to create. Some aquariums look stunning with minimal planting in a geological display dominated by rocks and bogwood, whereas others are totally plant filled, with no other decor visible among the foliage. Both displays can be equally effective, even though they are completely different. Or you may wish to recreate a natural habitat, such as a Southeast Asian stream, using only the plants and fish that are found together in the wild. In any case, it is always worthwhile to find out as much as possible about the plants you would like to use, including their ultimate size, their lighting requirements, and other environmental needs.

The sturdy leaves will survive the attention of boisterous or herbivorous fish.

This and other Anubias species can be grown attached to bogwood or rocks.

▲ Anubias barteri var. **barteri:** *This slow-growing, adaptable plant will make an impact wherever it is used. It reaches about 11.75 in. (30 cm) tall.*

▲ Anubias barteri var. **nana:** *This compact variety is ideal as a foreground plant, being only 4.75 in. (12 cm) high when mature. It will cope with dim lighting.*

▲ Bacopa caroliniana: *These small oval leaves contrast well with other leaf shapes. Provide bright light and plenty of plant food. It reaches up to 15.75 in. (40 cm).*

OTHER PLANT CHOICES

Alternanthera reineckii–up to 19.75 in. (50 cm)

Ammannia gracilis–9.75-19.75 in. (25-50 cm)

Anubias congensis–21.25 in. (54 cm)

Anubias gracilis–9.75-11.75 in. (25-30 cm)

Aponogeton species-11.75-25.5 in. (30-65 cm)

Bacopa monnieri–19.75 in. (50 cm)

Bacopa rotundifolia–15.75 in. (40 cm)

Cabomba aquatica–15.75 in. (40 cm)

Cardamine lyrata–13.75 in. (35 cm)

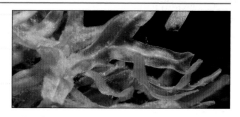

▲ *Algae (here coating the leaves) are simple plants that grow in the aquatic environment. They are usually out-competed for food and light by the more advanced plants, but you should take prompt action before they ruin the display (see page 53).*

This plant is often sold already attached to a piece of bogwood.

Keep the fine foliage free of debris.

▲ **Bolbitis heudelotii:** *This handsome slow-growing fern from Africa will thrive in areas of flowing water in the aquarium, growing up to 19.75 in. (50 cm) tall. It prefers bright lighting but is undemanding in terms of water conditions.*

▲ **Cabomba caroliniana:** *This is the most commonly available* Cabomba *species and the easiest to keep. It will cope with harder water and moderate light levels. It is fast growing, up to a height of 19.75 in. (50 cm).*

Aquarium plants (continued)

Generally speaking, a large plant should be placed behind a small one for obvious reasons, but plants can be grouped and placed in a number of ways to create an interesting design. Cryptocorynes are largely used for the fore- and midground of the aquarium, where they will spread and cover a large area if regularly propagated or divided. They are relatively hardy once settled, provided conditions are stable. A fine, heated substrate will improve plant health and encourage growth. Lighting requirements vary with each species, but many cryptocorynes are suited to low or subdued lighting. The larger *Echinodorus* species are ideal for the background of a spacious aquarium and, if given enough space and an open top, quickly produce leaves above the surface. If they become too tall, trim the roots and remove the taller leaves.

Lighting levels can affect the leaf color, from olive green to slightly brown.

This plant is large enough to split into two.

The common name of onion plant reflects the onion-shaped bulb from which the plant sprouts.

▲ **Crinum thaianum:** *The ribbonlike leaves of this stately plant can reach 5 ft. (150 cm) long, so place it with care in the display. The leaves are tough and so ideal for tanks housing large fish. This adaptable plant will flourish in a wide range of tank conditions.*

▲ **Cryptocoryne walkeri *var.* lutea:** *An easy-care plant that looks best in a group, it will grow up to 4.75 in. (12 cm) tall.*

▲ **Cryptocoryne wendtii:** *This useful plant can reach up to 13.75 in. (35 cm). It will grow fairly quickly into dense clumps.*

1 Remove the cryptocoryne from its pot and tease away the rockwool from the roots, then trim away any yellowing or damaged leaves.

2 Using the fingers of one hand, make a hollow in the substrate and gently push the plant in. Draw in substrate around the roots to anchor them.

3 You may find you need some extra substrate around the plants. Drop it gently into the tank. Continue planting, leaving enough space for growth.

These are sword plants from the Amazon region of South America. Many species are suitable for aquariums and will thrive with good light and generous feeding.

▲ **Echinodorus parviflorus:** *This compact sword plant (up to 9.75 in. [25 cm]) is ideal for small tanks. Feed it well.*

▲ **Echinodorus cordifolius:** *Trim this plant by removing large and older leaves. It grows up to 15.75 in.(40 cm) tall.*

▲ **Echinodorus 'Red Flame':** *A focal-point plant, it is easy to grow and will reach 15.75 in. (40 cm) or more.*

▲ **Echinodorus palaefolius var. latifolius:** *At 15.75 in. (40 cm) and taller, this makes a stately specimen.*

Aquarium plants (continued)

All plants need sufficient light to photosynthesize properly. In the aquarium, light has to be reproduced accurately to mimic the levels of light that plants would receive in their natural environments. Without the correct lighting, it is difficult to maintain aquarium plants successfully. Although lighting requirements do vary with individual species, most plants require more light than can be provided by a single fluorescent tube. Aquariums featuring a moderate number of plants normally need three or four fluorescent tubes, complete with reflectors, to bounce the maximum amount of light into the tank. To achieve the correct spectral output, a typical lighting setup could include two or three tubes designed for plant growth and a single full-spectrum tube to balance the visible light and create a more pleasing color.

If this adaptable plant is released into wild areas, it could swamp native plants.

Avoid placing this plant in shaded or covered areas.

▲ **Egeria densa:**
WARNING: This well-known plant is illegal in the United States. Always check state and federal laws before importing plants.

▲ **Glossostigma elatinoides:** *This tiny foreground plant will make a dense carpet, only .75 in. (2 cm) high, with bright lighting.*

▲ **Gymnocoronis spilanthoides:** *This is a vigorous plant up to 23.5 in. (60 cm) tall, with leaves reaching 5.5 in. (14 cm) long. It doesn't need a heated tank.*

◀ *Glossostigma elatinoides is a tiny foreground plant that requires careful handling.*

▶ *Before planting, remove as much of the rockwool as possible without damaging the plant.*

OTHER PLANT CHOICES

Ceratophyllum demersum–19.75 in. (50 cm)

Ceratopteris cornuta–13.75-19.75 in. (35-50 cm)

Didiplis diandra–9.75-13.75 in. (25-35 cm)

Eichhornia crassipes–11.75 in. (30 cm) spread

Eleocharis acicularis–6-9.75 in. (15-25 cm)

Eusteralis stellata–11.75-15.75 in. (30-40 cm)

Elodea canadensis–19.75 in. (50 cm) or more

Fontinalis antipyretica–spreading

Hydrocotyle verticillata–6-9.75 in. (15-25 cm)

AQUARIUM PLANTS

Prune any extended stems to maintain a dense appearance.

The unusual branching appearance of the leaves and stems makes this a distinctive plant in any aquarium. It will also grow in damp, boggy conditions.

▲ **Hemianthus micranthemoides:** *In small groups, this is ideal for midground areas. It grows up to 7.75 in. (20 cm) high.*

▲ **Heteranthera zosterifolia:** *This bushy plant, 19.75 in. (50 cm) tall, is ideal for the background. It grows short and bushy in bright, open areas.*

▲ **Hydrocotyle leucocephala:** *This fast-growing plant will quickly reach the surface in a 23.5 in. (60 cm)-deep tank, where the leaves will spread and shade plants below. Trim regularly to keep it in check. It is adaptable but best in bright light.*

Aquarium plants (continued)

Metal-halide, or halogen, lamps provide intense, high-output light via a tungsten filament. They are ideally suited to deeper aquariums, with a water depth of 23.5 in. (60 cm) or more. Suspended at least 11.75 in. (30 cm) above the aquarium to allow ample ventilation, a single unit will illuminate approximately 276.15 in.^{2} (1800 cm^2) of surface area (an aquarium 23.5 in. [60 cm] long and 11.75 in. [30 cm] wide). A 150-watt light should provide a suitable output for most aquariums, but you may need more than one lamp for aquariums longer than 39.5 in. (100 cm). Halogen lights are initially the most costly but provide the best output for demanding aquarium plants. These include plants that come from shallow, open areas or have red pigments that are less efficient at photosynthesis and so need more light. Plants with dark green leaves are adapted to low-light conditions and will not require bright light.

Taking cuttings from taller stems will produce a more bushy plant.

The veins of *Hygrophila polysperma* varieties are often white in color.

▲ **Hygrophila corymbosa:** *This popular and readily available aquarium plant is highly adaptable, relatively fast growing, and tolerant of a wide range of aquarium conditions. It grows up to 19.75 in. (50 cm) in height.*

▲ **Hygrophila polysperma:** *This has smaller leaves than H. corymbosa, in pale green to reddish-brown. It will grow to the same height as H. corymbosa.*

▲ **Ludwigia repens:** *This is an easy-care plant that will quickly grow 19.75 in. (50 cm) to the surface and spread across the surface.*

A HELPING HAND

Some red plants need an increased amount of light but may be too short to reach the surface regions. Use a plastic twist tie to secure them to the upper parts of a robust twiggy plant, such as *Hygrophila corymbosa* 'Stricta'. The attached plants will develop aerial roots but absorb most nutrients through their leaves.

▶ *The stem and leaves of* Myriophyllum tuberculatum *vary between brown and red. Strong lighting is essential.*

In the aquarium, good lighting is essential to keep this plant healthy.

▲ **Lysimachia nummularia:** *This is also a pond plant and is well suited to a cooler aquarium. It reaches 15.75 in. (40 cm).*

▲ **Monosolenium tenerum:** *This is a fernlike plant sold attached to rocks or stones. It creates a pad of foliage for fish to explore.*

▲ **Myriophyllum aquaticum:** *In bright light and soft water, this plant produces a luxuriant growth of fine feathery foliage up to 19.75 in. (50 cm) tall. Feed it with a multipurpose fertilizer, and keep the leaves free of visible debris.*

AQUARIUM PLANTS

Aquarium plants (continued)

When planning the aquarium, select a mixture of background, midground, and fore-ground plants, along with a few specimen and floating plants, if you wish. Most plants look best when grouped together, so there is no need to have a wide variety of species in the aquarium. Although it is tempting to use many different species, it is often a lot easier and more effective to use a limited number of species in larger groupings. And bear in mind that the planting should be suitable for the fish that live in the aquarium.

◀ **Pistia stratiotes**
This is a floating species with velvety leaves.

▶ **Salvinia natans**
Feathery roots take up nutrients and provide sanctuary for fish.

These leaves are really solid and can be .5 in. (1.5 cm) thick.

▲ **Microsorium pteropus:**
Java fern is easy to keep. It grows up to 9.75 in. (25 cm), attached to rocks or wood. The plant contains chemicals that deter most herbivorous fish from eating the leaves.

▲ **Sagittaria platyphylla:**
Given time, space, bright light, and iron, this 6–7.75 in. (15-20 cm) foreground plant will produce a dense carpet across the aquarium floor.

▲ **Vallisneria natans:**
This plant, reaching 19.75 in. (50 cm), is ideal for the background. The spiraling stem shown here bears a flower.

OTHER PLANT CHOICES

Lagarosiphon major–19.75 in. (50 cm)

Lilaeopsis novae-zelandiae–3-4 in. (8-10 cm)

Limnobium laevigatum–Floating

Limnophila sessiliflora–11.75-19.75 in. (30-50 cm)

Marsilea hirsuta–2 in. (5 cm)

Micranthemum umbrosum–11.75 in. (30 cm)

Nesaea crassicaulis–15.75-19.75 in. (40-50 cm)

Potamogeton crispus–up to 27.5 in. (70 cm)

Riccia fluitans–Floating

◀ *Tablet fertilizers are an alternative to liquid products. Use them to feed particular plants or when the laterite in the substrate is exhausted. Place the tablet near the plant roots, and push it into the substrate.*

AQUARIUM PLANTS

The twisted leaves provide a contrast to the flat leaves of other varieties.

These clay plant stones covered in Java moss are commonly available from suppliers.

▲ **Vallisneria tortifolia:** *With a maximum height of 9.75 in. (25 cm), this undemanding, adaptable plant is ideal for small aquariums.*

▲ **Vesicularia dubyana:** *Java moss attaches to any hard surface and spreads in all directions. Trim it regularly to keep it in shape.*

▲ **Vallisneria spiralis 'Tiger':** *This easy-care plant has thinner leaves than the natural form. It grows fast in bright light, up to 23.5 in. (60 cm) tall.*

Mountain stream

At the source of a river, the water is clear, well oxygenated, and low in organic load. The number of fish species in these habitats is limited, but those that do live here survive against the odds and manage to find abundant food despite the harsh environment. They have adapted to both slow-moving water and raging, powerful flows, depending on the time of year. Life is also hard for the plants in this rocky environment. The only plant submerged in the tank water is Java moss (*Vesicularia dubyana*). Alpine plants will thrive in rock crevices above the waterline, and houseplants can simulate overhanging foliage.

*This tank uses a silver sand substrate, but medium-grade gravel would also work well. Ensure that the substrate can support heavy rockwork safely. Medium-grade pea gravel is grouped in some areas, as if the water flow has separated it from finer sand.

▲ Large, angular pieces of slate convey the powerful feel of the waterfall. The smaller, rounded pieces look as if they have broken away and been smoothed by the constant erosion of flowing water.

The overhanging leaves of houseplants above or behind the aquarium imitate terrestrial vegetation.

This piece of bogwood represents a sunken tree root.

These large rocks are heavy and sharp and could be dangerous if not attached firmly in place.

Smaller, rounded slate pieces scattered across the substrate continue the rocky feel.

BOGWOOD AND PLANTS

A few pieces of bogwood soften the overall look but are not vital and are best used as finishing touches. Wood with Java moss attached adds a hint of plant life. Conditions in the rocky mountain stream are unfavorable for plant growth, so in this display, the planting is confined to alpine plants above the water.

FILTRATION

To convey the water movement and rocky surroundings typically found in this environment, it helps to be able to see the water coming into the tank. This can be achieved by filling only two-thirds of the aquarium and constructing a waterfall at one end. A sufficiently powerful pump will produce a strong flow of water.

▲ Bogwood pieces and alpine plants (Sedum *and* Arenaria) make ideal decor.

▲ *A shoal of zebra danios will look at home in this aquarium and relish the fast-flowing water. They will tolerate coolness.*

Direct the flow of water carefully over the rocks to create a lively impact without too much splashing.

The open water area is perfect for the fish to swim against the flow, while the rockwork provides quiet retreats.

SUITABLE FISH

Most mountain stream fish are small, with streamlined bodies, such as the White Cloud Mountain minnow *(Tanichthys albonubes)*. Nearly all are relatively peaceful and constantly active. Many barbs are ideally suited to a fast-flowing environment, as is another popular aquarium fish, the zebra danio *(Brachydanio rerio)*.

Central American river

The rivers of Central America are often clean and clear, flowing over exposed rock. In some places, the fast-flowing waters are interspersed with calmer areas of flat land that often form substantial pools. Fish hide and breed in small pockets around the margins.

SUBSTRATE

Smooth pea gravel will support the weight of the large slate rocks and protect the mouths of digging fish. To prevent this behavior from undermining the rockwork, place the majority of the substrate on the base of the tank, with a mesh covering on top. Place the rocks on the mesh, followed by the remainder of the gravel.

▲ The large, bold rocks in this display would look artificial against the pea gravel. Using small pieces of the same rock type around the base of the larger pieces blends the two together. Make sure that all rockwork is secured with silicone sealant.

*The cichlids suited to this aquarium are very messy eaters that create a lot of waste. Be sure to install adequate filtration to maintain consistently good water quality in the tank, and clean the substrate regularly with an aquarium gravel cleaner.

Large upright rocks can be attached to the aquarium glass with silicone.

Java fern (though not from Central America) will produce baby plants from its leaves. You can remove these and wedge them into cracks in the rockwork, where they will root and spread.

You could use a layer of fine- or medium-grade pea gravel below the mesh covering and medium- or large-grade gravel above.

Position large rocks to create caves and hiding places that fish may use for breeding.

WOOD AND PLANTS

The wood used here acts as a rooting medium for one plant, a Java fern variety called *Microsorium pteropus* 'Windelov' (below). It will withstand the attentions of herbivorous or destructive cichlids. If its feathered leaves are torn by fish, the effect is less noticeable. Large *Echinodorus* and *Sagittaria* species are alternative choices.

▶ *A male firemouth cichlid lives up to its name, with a fiery show of red to ward off intruders.*

▲ *The South American banded leporinus adds a striking pattern to the tank.*

◀ *Algae-eating catfish such as this Hypostomus sp. will mix with cichlids.*

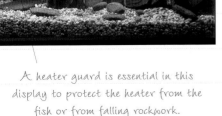

A heater guard is essential in this display to protect the heater from the fish or from falling rockwork.

SUITABLE FISH

These waters are home to many fish, including some of the popular cichlids and other large species that often exhibit territorial and aggressive tendencies. Suitable fish include the firemouth cichlid *(Thorichthys meeki)* and the banded leporinus *(Leporinus fasciatus)*.

Flooded Amazon forest

During the rainy season in the Amazon, there comes a point when the river can no longer hold the massive influx of water. It bursts its banks and spreads over a wide expanse, creating a whole new world for its aquatic inhabitants. In the aquarium, overhanging vegetation and forest debris across the substrate evoke the natural environment.

Black gravel helps create a darker, more textured substrate.

This planting medium resembles the mulm that accumulates on the flooded forest floor.

The unusual color of Alternanthera reineckii blends well with the wood and debris in the aquarium.

BOGWOOD

Select pieces of bogwood that look like fallen or broken branches. Larger pieces can represent tree roots. If you can find a suitably large round piece, place small plants around the base to create a major feature in the aquarium. Wash bogwood thoroughly before use to remove tannins, but a slight brown tinge to the water can add to the overall effect. Some items of artificial decor are designed to look like tree stumps and are ideal for this display. Use them to hide filters, heaters, and other aquarium equipment.

▲
To overcome the buoyancy of bark, use silicone to glue pieces to a sheet of glass on the tank base.

The cork bark along the center of the display is a main item of decor and helps create the forest floor appearance.

FLOODED AMAZON FOREST

PLANTS

In this design, there are two clear planting areas, one at the surface and one on the substrate. If possible, keep the two separate, with swimming space in between. Plants with twiglike stalks and a terrestrial appearance will give the impression of flooded land plants. Choose low-growing foreground plants on the bottom and floating plants for the surface. Alternatively, hang some twigs or plastic plants from above to represent overhanging foliage.

▶ *This synthetic plant represents overhanging foliage in the aquarium.*

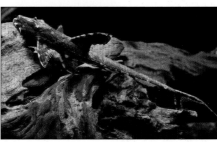

Small floating plants, such as water lettuce (Pistia stratiotes), will mix well with some artificial plants to create the effect of leaves from terrestrial plants dipping into the water. This will help to block out excessive light and provide a retreat for fish.

◀ *Angelfish (Pterophyllum scalare) will thrive in this setup, spending time in the upper reaches.*

Mopani wood has a rough texture and makes an interesting hiding spot for bottom-dwelling catfish.

▲ *Whiptail catfish, such as* Rineloricaria lanceolata, *will appreciate the hiding spots provided by the wood and vegetation.*

SUITABLE FISH

The flooded forest is home to the fish normally found in the affected rivers. Shoaling fish such as cardinal, black widow, and rummy-nose tetras will swim in midwater. Angelfish are ideal for the upper areas, and many catfish will live on the aquarium floor.

Congo whitewater river

Much of the Congo River in central Africa is surrounded by tropical rain forest, and in the lower reaches, the waters are calm and sandy. However, farther upstream, the Congo carves through solid rock, creating white-water rapids that appear inhospitable to any life. Nevertheless, fish are found in the turbulent stretches, thriving in the oxygenated water.

THE SUBSTRATE

The riverbed is a mixture of sand and gravel-like substrate. The turbulent flow in the rapids lifts much of the sandy substrate, creating water with high levels of suspended particles and very low visibility. The sand used in this display will need regular stirring to prevent compaction and the buildup of anaerobic conditions. In time, it will need replacing.

▲ Large angular pieces of slate can be complemented by smaller slate chippings scattered across the aquarium floor. Debris collecting on a sandy substrate is easy to remove using a siphon.

*Air pumps, powerheads, and an external filter are combined to create the impression of a strong water flow. Some air line without an airstone produces large, rising bubbles.

The tough, crinkled leaves of Crinum natans are unusual and well equipped to cope with strong flows of water. They will soon grow to the water surface.

This large piece of slate divides the aquarium into distinct areas.

Java moss (Vesicularia dubyana)

▼ *Congo tetras (Phenacogrammus interruptus) can be found shoaling in the calmer spots between rapids and will enjoy a little water movement in the aquarium.*

▲ *Many scavenging catfish, such as this* Synodontis angelicus, *live in the region and will thrive, albeit nocturnally, in the tank.*

▼ Distichodus, *here the round-faced D. sexfasciatus, lives in the waters of Africa's Zaire Basin and will bring a distinctive, if aggressive, presence to the tank.*

SUITABLE FISH

This is a habitat rich in bottom dwellers (catfish and loaches), rock dwellers (cichlids), and open-water swimmers (tetras and barbs). These will create a lively display in which all areas of the aquarium are occupied. You can also choose from many more fish from similar habitats in other regions.

African fern (*Bolbitis heudelotii*) appreciates the strong water flow.

Slate pieces are laid horizontally as though they had fallen or broken away from the underlying rock.

▲ *Reasonable lighting and a few nutrients are all that the slow-growing* Anubias barteri *var.* nana *requires. In the aquarium, African fern and Java moss are added to the wood to dramatic effect.*

Lake Malawi

The crystal-clear waters of Lake Malawi lap against alternating rocky and sandy shore-lines, and the shoals of beautifully colored fish can be clearly seen just beneath the surface. The lake is home to more than 600 cichlid species, most of them unique to the lake. Many species occur only in certain locations within the lake.

THE ROCKWORK

Rounded boulders of varying sizes re-create the natural habitat in this display. Apart from two very large rocks, most of the pieces are about 7.75 in. (20 cm) in diameter or less. Smaller rocks and pebbles are used on the aquarium floor and to fill some gaps in the rockwork. Use silicone sealant to fix the rocks in position before filling the tank; you must be certain that they are stable and secure.

▶ *Silver sand is an ideal base to support the heavy rockwork. Make the sand layer at least 3 in. (about 7.5 cm) deep across the entire base.*

* Before building up a rockwork display, make sure the aquarium will be able to house the weight. Lava or tufa rock are porous and therefore lightweight choices.

▲ *In nature, the rocks would lie as they had fallen; try to re-create this impression in the aquarium.*

WATER QUALITY

Provide hard, alkaline, and stable water conditions. To cope with the quantities of waste produced by the fish, use one or more external filters, and include plenty of mechanical and biological filter media.

Use a plastic mesh covering to prevent digging cichlids from undermining the rocks.

Rocks broken in half create the impression of partially buried boulders.

◀ *This is a male Trewavas's mbuna* (Labeotropheus trewavasae), *a common inhabitant of Lake Malawi. Beneath the droop nose, the mouth contains rows of tiny rasping teeth used to scrape food from rocks.*

▼ *Zebra cichlids* (Metriaclima *sp.*) *are also mbuna, rock dwellers from Lake Malawi. Note the egg spots.*

* A dense mat of algal fuzz, known as aufwuchs, covers the rocks and is home to many tiny creatures that form the basis of the fish's food. In the aquarium, they accept most proprietary foods.

LAKE MALAWI

A mixture of shapes, sizes, and tones creates a varied rockscape.

The sand is deeper here to support the heavier rocks.

SUITABLE FISH

The fish that inhabit the lake can be divided into two groups: the rock-dwelling fish, or mbuna, and the open-water fish, often called haps. Of most interest to the aquarist are the rock dwellers. These are found all around the lake, often near the surface, where food is readily available around the large, rounded boulders and rocks that make up the typical rocky areas. In any particular rocky area, swarms of fish thrive beneath the surface. Suitable genera include *Melanochromis, Labeotropheus,* and *Metriaclima*.

Southeast Asian swamp

The swamps of Southeast Asia could be described as an underwater jungle. Dense aquatic foliage covers every available space, creating a habitat for small labyrinth fish (anabantoids) and rasboras. This is an ideal setting to re-create in the aquarium.

THE SUBSTRATE

Create a rooting medium for the plants by layering substrates. A typical mix would be a layer of silver sand, preferably around a heating cable, followed by a fine lime-free substrate mixed with, or containing, a layer of nutrient-rich substrate additive.

THE PLANTS

The most important aspect of this display is the large number of plants. Bushy species, trimmed to varying lengths, are ideal for the middle-to-foreground area. Taller, unusual plants can occupy the midground and background zones.

Bamboo canes, cut to different lengths and placed randomly among the plants, help create a swamplike environment. Replace these frequently.

◀ *The leaves of Pistia stratiotes have a velvety texture. Fine, trailing roots are produced below the surface.*

Place feathery leaved plants, such as Cabomba, in areas of gentle water flow to prevent clogging from debris.

Rocks divide planting areas and help define individual groups of plants.

A few shorter plants with large leaves cover areas of substrate but leave swimming space above.

Silver sand looks good, but a mixture of substrates provides more plant nutrients.

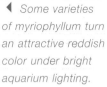

◀ Some varieties of myriophyllum turn an attractive reddish color under bright aquarium lighting.

◀ Trim dense, bushy plants, such as Heteranthera zosterifolia (from South America), so that they are shorter toward the front of the aquarium.

▶ The thick, rounded leaves of Lobelia cardinalis contrast well with bushy plants.

▼ This style of aquarium is an ideal environment for a male Siamese fighting fish (Betta splendens).

◀ Often hidden from view, the kuhli loach helps reduce algae and remove waste.

Untidy plants create a more natural, swamplike display.

SUITABLE FISH

Many popular aquarium fish originate from the Southeast Asian swamps, including gouramis, catfish, loaches, barbs, and rasboras. The gouramis are well suited to this setup and will appreciate the densely planted display. Good choices include pearl, opaline, and moonlight gouramis. Shoalers such as harlequin rasboras will flourish in open water areas, and the fascinating, if elusive, kuhli loach will occupy the lower regions.

Picture credits

Additional picture credits

The publishers would like to thank the following photographers for providing images, credited here by page number and position: T(Top), B(Bottom), C(Center), BL(Bottom left), etc.

Aqua Press (M-P & C. Piednoir): 69(TL)

Photomax (Max Gibbs): 48(T)

The information and recommendations in this book are given without any guarantees on the part of the author and publisher, who disclaim any liability with the use of this material.